The Graphic Gospel: Preaching in a Postliterate Age

Jay Richard Akkerman

Academy of Preachers *Books*,
Dwight A. Moody, General Editor
Dissertation Series

Academy of Preachers Books

The Graphic Gospel: Preaching in a Postliterate Age

ISBN: Softcover 978-0692574188
Copyright © 2015 by Jay Richard Akkerman

All rights reserved. No part of this book may be reproduced or transmitted in any form or by any means, electronic or mechanical, including photocopying, recording, or by any information storage and retrieval system, without permission in writing from the publisher.

To order additional copies of this book, contact:

Parson's Porch & Company
1-423-475-7308
www.parsonsporch.com

Academy of Preachers Books is an imprint of Parson's Porch & Company (PP&C) in Cleveland, Tennessee. PP&C is an innovative organization which raises money by publishing books of noted authors, representing all genres. All donations from contributors and profits from publishing are shared with the poor.

The Graphic Gospel:
Preaching in a Postliterate Age

Jay Richard Akkerman

ABSTRACT

The purpose of the study was to determine which factors related to congregational receptivity toward the use of visual media in preaching by exploring factors including generational group, gender, dogmatism, postmodernism, and postliteracy. The study consisted of a researcher-designed, cross-sectional quantitative survey of attitudes toward the use of visual media in preaching. The survey was completed by 113 respondents age fourteen or older at New Hope Community Church of the Nazarene in Tempe, Arizona. The research findings contradicted the popularly held notion tying age to receptivity toward visual media, and underscored the importance of pastoral integrity in a visual hermeneutic.

DISSERTATION APPROVAL

This is to certify that the dissertation titled

THE GRAPHIC GOSPEL:

PREACHING IN A POSTLITERATE AGE

presented by

Jay Richard Akkerman

has been accepted toward fulfillment

of the requirements for the

DOCTOR OF MINISTRY degree at

Asbury Theological Seminary

Kenneth A. Boyd Mentor	December 3, 2003 Date
[signature] Internal Reader	December 3, 2003 Date
Leslie A. Andrews Vice President for Educational Development	December 3, 2003 Date

THE GRAPHIC GOSPEL:

PREACHING IN A POSTLITERATE AGE

A Dissertation

Presented to the Faculty of

Asbury Theological Seminary

In Partial Fulfillment

Of the Requirements for the Degree

Doctor of Ministry

by

Jay Richard Akkerman

May 2004

TABLE OF CONTENTS

List of Tables 15
List of Figures 16
Acknowledgements 17
Preface 21

Chapter One: Overview of the Study 25

    Background 25
    The Problem 26
    Secular Models 28
        Print Media 28
        Television Media 29
    Purpose 30
    Research Questions 30
        Research Question #1 31
        Research Question #2 31
        Research Question #3 31
        Research Question #4 31
        Research Question #5 31
    Definition of Terms 31
        Preaching 31
        Dogmatism 32
        Electronic Media 32
        Iconism and Aniconism 34
        Modernism and Modernity 34
        Postmodernism and Postmodernity 35
        Postliteracy 39
    Historical and Theological Foundations 40
    Context of the Project 44
    Description of the Project 46
    Methodology 46
    Variables 47
    Instrumentation and Data Collection 47
    Delimitations and Generalizability 47
    Population 48
    Importance 48
    Overview of the Dissertation 49

Chapter Two: Precedents in the Literature 50

Biblical and Theological Precedents 51
- Old Testament Forms 52
- New Testament Forms 53
- Ecclesiastical Precedents 61
- Literary Precedents 76
- Forms of Literacy 77
- Homiletical Precedents 81
- Conclusion 88

Chapter Three: Design of the Study 90

Problem and Purpose 90
Hypothesis 90
Research Questions 90
- Research Question #1 90
- Research Question #2 90
- Research Question #3 91
- Research Question #4 91
- Research Question #5 91
Research Methodology 91
- Population and Sample 91
- Variables 92
- Instrumentation 92
- Pilot Testing 97
- Data Collection 97
Data Analysis 98

Chapter Four: Findings of the Study 100

Respondent Profiles 100
Openness to Change 103
Postmodernism 105
Media Receptivity 108
Media Subscales 109
Research Question #4 113
Research Question #5 120
- Gender 120
- Attendance 120
- Tenure 121

- Commitment 121
- Summary of Significant Findings 122
  - Demographic Characteristics 122
  - Parishioner Characteristics 123
  - Dogmatic Characteristics 123
  - Postliterate Characteristics 123

Chapter Five: Summary and Conclusions 125

- Major Findings 125
  - Demographic Characteristics 125
  - Parishioner Characteristics 126
  - Dogmatic Characteristics 127
  - Postliterate Characteristics 128
- Research Questions and Answers 129
  - Research Question #1 129
  - Research Question #2 129
  - Research Question #3 130
  - Research Question #4 130
  - Research Question #5 131
- Limitations of the Study 131
- Implications of the Findings and Practical Applications 132
  - Media as an Apostolic Successor of Image Bearing 132
  - Media as a Contextual Carrier of Biblical Metaphors 133
  - Media as Cultural Language 134
- Contributions to Research Methodology 134
- Suggestions for Further Study 135
- Postscript 136

Appendix A 138

- Cover Letter 138
- Section One 140
- Section Two 143
- Section Three 147
- Section Four 149

Appendix B 152
Appendix C 154
Appendix D 157
Works Cited 159

LIST OF TABLES

Table 1. Twentieth Century Generations in the United States 43
Table 2. Jesus' Direct Use of Visual Object Lessons 56
Table 3. Jesus' Use of Metaphor 58
Table 4. Key to Postmodern Values Questionnaire 97
Table 5. Modified Respondent Age 101
Table 6. Respondent Tenure at New Hope Church 102
Table 7. Respondent Attendance at New Hope Church 103
Table 8. Listing of Dissertation Survey Scales 104
Table 9. Dogmatism Scores by Generational Group 105
Table 10. Postmodern Subjectivity Subscale 107
Table 11. Postmodern Subjectivity Subscale Scores by Generational Group 108
Table 12. Media Scale Scores by Generation 109
Table 13. Pastoral Media Subscale 110
Table 14. Correlation of Variables in Analysis 112
Table 15. Media Imagery Subscale 113
Table 16. Crosstab on Memory Triggers 114
Table 17. Crosstab on News Media Preference 115
Table 18. News Media Preference and Dogmatism 116
Table 19. Crosstab on Sermon Retention 117
Table 20. Regression on Pastoral Media Subscale 119
Table 21. Regression on Media Imagery Subscale 120
Table 22. Commitment and Media Receptivity 122

LIST OF FIGURES

Figure 1. *Biblia Pauperum Blockbook* Template..66

Figure 2. Christ Is Crucified 69

Figure 3. MasterWorks: The Maker's Mark..85

Figure 4. *Pietà* Inscription: Michelangelo Buonarroti From Florence Made This 87

Figure 5. Insert Name Here..88

ACKNOWLEDGEMENTS

I offer my deepest appreciation to:

Dr. Ken Boyd. Your willingness to serve as my mentor and your tenacious encouragement of my work inspired me to continue, even when my goal of completion seemed incomprehensible at times. Words cannot express my thanks for your friendship and support.

Dr. Joel Green. Your relentless pursuit of biblical truth and your prolific theological writings inspired me to break through many writer's blocks long after the midnight hour. Thank you for your thoughtful exploration of my writing and your willingness to serve on my committee.

Dr. Leslie Andrews. For the countless times you welcomed me into your office to help focus my thinking, I express my deepest thanks. You are a gifted educator with an incredible heart for ministry. Thank you for challenging me to see this project through and to recognize its value for the Church at-large.

Dr. Tom Tumblin. Although I was disappointed that you were not able to remain on my committee, I give thanks for the many times you answered my questions, challenged my thoughts, and encouraged me to stay the course in conveying the gospel in graphic terms. Your support is greatly appreciated.

Dr. Dale Galloway and Dr. Ellsworth Kalas. Without question, my year under your teaching shaped my life and ministry in ways I cannot yet fully grasp. My family and I will be forever grateful for the incredibly generous support of the Beeson Center and its staff, offering particular recognition to the stellar work of Penny Ruot. I also offer my sincere thanks to Dr. Kalas for his unyielding demand that I remain true to the biblical text we both love so much. As a reformed Strip Miner, by your stripes, I'm healed.

Dr. Chuck McKinney. Your open door and readiness to pray on my behalf have been more important to me than you will ever know. I thank you and Zoe for opening your home to me in Flagstaff, and I pray for the new work he is bringing to life through your lives, leadership, and ministry. God bless you both.

My fellow Beeson pastors from the class of 1998-99. I give thanks to

God for the ways he has shaped me through the friendships of my fellow Strip Miners Donna Bartleson-Manwaring, Tory Baucum, Stan Cardwell, Dr. Rick Danielson, Dwight Gregory, Jeff Heath, Dr. Chris Heckaman, Alex Lupo, Dr. David Munguia, Solomon Muwanga, Dr. Vance Rains, Dr. Brian Rainwater, Dr. Dan Reinhardt, Silas Ripato, Dr. Alan Robinson, Dr. Lou Shirey, Dr. Andy Snodgrass, Carness Vaughan, and Chris Volz. You have left an indelible mark on the life of our family. We are eternally grateful for your friendship.

The congregation of believers called New Hope Community Church of the Nazarene. By God's grace and your faithfulness, you graphically lived up to your name: a community experiencing new hope. I give thanks for all your support, and for the privilege of serving as your pastor. New Hope's greatest days are undoubtedly yet ahead.

The members of my research and reflection team. Dr. Will Brown, Dr. Glenn Chaffee, Darlene Coleman, Marilee Naeve, Barbara Schumacher, Margie Shannon, and Dan Shook all contributed countless hours meeting with me, praying for this project, proofreading the text, and especially encouraging me in the journey. Special thanks go to Dr. Will Brown, whose statistical knowledge and expertise in using SPSS were invaluable. Thank you for patiently teaching me how to analyze my findings. This dissertation is clearly the product of your partnership in this regard.

Brad Wiggers and Curtis Pierce. As key members of New Hope's weekly design team, it has been a pleasure to dream and scheme with you about how to communicate the gospel in creative, compelling ways. You have made our challenge each week a great adventure.

The administration of Northwest Nazarene University and the faculty of its School of Theology and Christian Ministries. I give thanks for the ways you have shaped my ministry across the years and pray that I will faithfully pass the torch of this graphic gospel on to the students you now call me to teach as a member of your faculty.

Aaron Knapp, Randall Davey, and Dr. Jeff Crosno. Your models of ministry continue to inspire me after all these years. Thank you for serving as my pastors across the years and for offering me personal models of what it means to be a faithful preacher.

My mother, Mary Akkerman, and my brother Mark Akkerman. You are the two most creative people I have ever known. I am blessed by your love and your creative example. I only wish Dad could have lived to see this day.

Lauren, Hailey, and Parker Akkerman. We are blessed by three wonderfully wonder-filled girls, and I thank God daily for each of you. To Lauren, our oldest, and Hailey and Parker, our Asbury twins who have never known their father without this dissertation looming large in the background, I have only one thing to say: we're going to Disneyland!

Kim Akkerman. I save the best for last. Without your constant love, sacrifice, and dedication, this dissertation would never have been completed. Together, God has taken two kids from Idaho to places we never dreamed possible, and I wouldn't want to travel a day of the journey without you. I dedicate this work to you, my best friend and partner for life, with all my love.

PREFACE

In the fourth century, Athens was still the leading center of late classical Greek culture. Students came from all over Asia Minor, Egypt and North Africa to study with one particular professor. These students included some of the greatest theologians in the history of Christianity, including Gregory of Nazianzus and Basil of Caesarea.

The name of the professor was Prohairesius, an Armenian Christian who refused to remove himself from Greek culture and its educational structures, unlike the monks. Instead, he sought to embed the teaching of the gospel in Greek eusebia (spiritual formation) and paideia (academic inquiry).

When Prohairesius gave his inaugural lecture as professor of rhetoric, a large audience gathered along with the Roman provincial governor. Even though it was a command performance, Prohairesius walked in and announced he had prepared nothing in particular, but was prepared for anything and everything. He invited his defeated rivals for the academic chair to choose a topic for him. When they announced their chosen topic, Prophairesius turned visibly pale, his color contrasting sharply with his blond hair and strikingly handsome physique.

He then asked the governor for two small favors. At first the governor was not amused, but decided to play along with what Greek rhetoricians called an epideixis—a dazzling display-piece, a vehicle to show off the professor's undoubted brilliance at pulling out the rabbit from the hat.

These were Prohairesius' two requests. First, no applause until the end. Second, would the best shorthand writer available transcribe his address?

The governor decided to humor Prohairesius and keep the drama of the "epideixis" going. Prohairesius began his inaugural speech, and the shorthand expert began the transcription. Prohairesius' reasoning was impeccable, his delivery flawless, his style elegant. The audience had obviously been won over. But when Prohairesius came to the Part II of his speech, he reversed engines and proceeded to rebut and destroy all the arguments he had just made in Part I.

It was all the audience could do to refrain from applause at this tour de force. Prohairesius stilled his admirers with his hand, dismissing his performance as prosaic, only what anyone should be able to do who was occupying a chair of such importance to both eusebia and paideia.

Prohairesius instructed the shorthand expert to pay strict attention. He would give the speech again, word for word. If any deviation from the first speech, the shorthand expert was to interrupt him and call him out. After all, the king of intellect was memory. Prohairesius delivered the entire oration again, without missing one word or one pause. When he was finished, the audience applauded enthusiastically, kissed the new professor's chest and feet, "while his humbled rivals groveled disheveled on the dusty ground, though even in that position they too joined in the applause."

Already by the fourth century, preachers had become laborers of points and performers of words rather than painters of pictures and tellers of stories. This was a long journey from Jesus the storyteller in a very short time.

The rediscovery of Jesus the story-teller is one of the most significant homiletic developments of the past half century. We are only beginning to realize how much the church has tamed, westernized, intellectualized, gentrified Jesus, whose stories and teachings were once scandalous and shocking, counterintuitive and countercultural. But there is much debate over the best way for preachers to tell the Jesus story today, and to what extent should that story be told using digital visual media.

A lot of wrong turns and miss-steps over the past couple of decades could have been avoided (not to mention entire books and conferences canceled) if Jay Akkerman's splendid 2003 dissertation had been more accessible and studied. With scrupulous scholarship and methodological savvy, Akkerman slowly builds the case for four stunning conclusions.

First, preachers today stand in an "apostolic succession of image-bearers" that started with Jesus and that "carry the torch of creative communication" for the church today.

Second, psychographics is more important than demographics (whether generation, gender or other identity markers) when it comes to openness to and literacy about digital visual media.

Third, the introduction of visuals into worship in and of itself does not make a better sermon. Preaching still rises and falls on the preacher, not on tools or techniques. Preaching is less about the state of the sermon than the state of the preacher.

Finally, the use of visual media is not some magic wand for evangelism, either in terms of reaching younger generations or for reaching the "nones" (unchurched) and "dones" (de-churched). The introduction into worship of visual media is only one ingredient in a complex of factors that make "live worship." The highest aim in preaching is not to razzle-dazzle with visuals or supply apps to try out for the next week, but to release the powers of holiness that come for the Holy Spirit; not offer fixed solutions, but open a fountain which flows deep and wide.

What is clear from Akkerman's pioneering research is that preachers have stressed the Bible as a source of the language of faith and the philosophy of truth, like Prohairesius, and not stressed enough the Bible as source of the stories and metaphors and songs of faith. The key is telling the story with passion and power, a telling which can take many shapes and forms. To our peril preachers take the fire out of hell, the gold out of heaven, the blood out of the altar, the divine out of the human, the saint out of the sinner.

Most important of all, and this applies to both preacher and pew, the story is something we walk not just talk. The more I inhabit the story of Jesus, the more the story of Jesus inhabits me.

Leonard Sweet, Drew University, George Fox University, Tabor College, preachthestory.com

CHAPTER ONE

OVERVIEW OF THE STUDY

Background

"I AM here, too." These four words from the Holy Spirit resonated deeply in Glenn Chaffee's heart within minutes of his first arrival as a guest at New Hope Community Church of the Nazarene. Even a few years after his first visit, Glenn still considers this sentence the most direct impression he has received from God in roughly three-quarters of a century.

When I first welcomed Glenn and Rachael Chaffee into the church's rented middle school cafeteria in March 2000, I was certain their first visit would also be their last. After all, the Chaffees were much older than nearly everyone in the small congregation at that time. They dressed more conservatively than anyone else, and I highly doubted they would appreciate the church's styles of media, not to mention the volume of its music. My assumptions were incorrect in nearly every respect. In fact, the Chaffees became faithful weekly attenders at New Hope, eventually becoming members and active ministry leaders.

Despite New Hope's use of visual media in worship, despite the lack of overt emphasis on denominational distinctives, despite the annoying challenges of setting up and tearing down a portable church in a middle school cafeteria every week, God reminded Glenn and Rachael of his presence in a church that was very different from any other they had known before. Over time, other senior adults began attending New Hope with increasing regularity. Some who formerly attended the church under the founding pastor's leadership returned. Others came through the invitation of friends and family.

"I don't know why you like our church so much," I joked with these older attenders, "but I'm sure glad you're here!" God was at work at New Hope in people of all ages.

Without a doubt, my ministry will be forever in debt to the Beeson International Center for Biblical Preaching and Church Leadership at Asbury Theological Seminary. The Beeson Center is recognized as one of the Church's premiere training grounds for advanced pastoral leadership training in the Wesleyan tradition. During my course work at Asbury's campus in Wilmore, Kentucky, the Beeson Center was led by Dr. Dale Galloway, its dean. Dr. Galloway has extensive pastoral leadership experience in several regions of the country, including success in planting two megachurches: Grove City Church of the Nazarene in Grove City, Ohio and New Hope Community Church, a nondenominational church in Portland, Oregon. Under Dr. Galloway's leadership, the Beeson Center is modeled after the war college: pastors who show leadership promise are gathered together from around the world for a year of intensive study and exposure to leading-edge ministry models. All of this is done in hopes of sending these pastors back into ministry with greater overall effectiveness earlier in their careers.

During my residential year at Asbury, my class traveled to many leading American evangelical churches, including Saddleback Valley Community Church in Lake Forest, California, Willow Creek Community Church in South Barrington, Illinois, Ginghamsburg United Methodist Church in Tipp City, Ohio, and Peachtree Presbyterian and Perimeter churches in the Atlanta, Georgia, metroplex. In addition to an international trip to Jordan, Israel, and Egypt, we also traveled to South Korea. In Seoul, we were guests of Bishop Sundo Kim, pastor of Kwang Lim, the largest Methodist church in the world, and Pastor Paul Yonggi Cho of the Yoido Full Gospel Church, the world's largest Protestant church with nearly one million members.

Thanks to the Beeson program, I witnessed firsthand an emphasis on creative communication and outreach methods to those who were not yet followers of Christ. Contemporary Christian music, coupled with dynamic uses of visual media, seemed to connect powerfully with the disconnected of my generation. Having used a variety of lower-tech media forms in my previous church, I found my horizons expanded at Asbury and determined to adopt these new methods upon the completion of my Beeson year. From my first Sunday at New Hope, I employed visual media in my preaching. The use of visual media quickly became prevalent in weekly worship. Today media is a normative element at New Hope, not to mention a primary signature of the church's Sunday morning worship encounters each week.

The Problem

Since coming to New Hope, God surprised me many times with those who made New Hope their church home. In hindsight, I wrongly presumed that New Hope's worship style and commitments to technology connected almost exclusively with younger people. Instead, the church has seen people of all ages embrace their faith in Christ through these multidimensional communication forms. I became interested in learning why older adults, who have lived most of their lives from a modern worldview, connected with my preaching when it intentionally adopts what I considered postmodern methods of delivery. This interest led me to consider whether the essentials of preaching to younger generations today are really unique, or if they are transgenerational.

A decade or two before Dick Clark broadcast his grand millennium celebration from New York's Time Square on 31 December 1999, the effects of postmodernism were already emerging across generations. Clark, who is himself a member of the Builder generation and a favorite of many Baby Boomers, led Americans of all ages in ushering in the millennium countdown hour-by-hour. From the international dateline and with hourly coverage from each successive time zone, Clark's broadcast vividly demonstrated the turn of the millennium in visual terms. In the same way that his story was transcontinental, his audience was transgenerational.

Today the impact of media technologies permeates most of American culture, affecting not only those born since its advent. All Americans live under its influence. Video screens compete for the attention of all ages in grocery stores, libraries, and even at gasoline pumps. Television commercials now feature Senior citizens transmitting and capturing video images on cellular phones from their millennial grandchildren. Personal digital assistants and wireless technologies make communications portable as well as visual. The world is becoming ever more linked into a global video network, yet even in the early years of the twenty-first-century, much of the Church's preaching continues to center on the audio channel rather than utilizing a more interactive, multidimensional spectrum. To illustrate, *Preaching* magazine awarded its book of the year for 2001 to Graham Johnston's *Preaching to a Postmodern World*. However, old habits apparently die hard since the book was subtitled *A Guide to Reaching Twenty-First Century Listeners*. Apparently, many in the Church find it difficult to conceive of preaching involving anything other than a speaker and hearers.

Regardless of the era, human communication is culturally linked. Effective communication requires a connection between a sender and receiver to ensure the transmission of ideas. A blind man cannot communicate effectively with a deaf woman until he finds a common means of relay. Likewise, a Brazilian woman who does not read, write, or speak French must find some common ground to place an order with her Parisian waiter. At its most basic level, effective communication is all about making connections between people. Likewise, the following secular communication principles have been at work in the communities of God's gathered people as well, regardless of their age or demographic makeup.

Secular Models

Print Media

A survey of secular models may offer preachers insight into how and why other media forms have transitioned toward more visual forms.

USA Today. On Friday, 29 February 1980, Allen Neuharth, chair of Gannett newspaper group, gathered with members of a secret task force known only as "Project NN" for a clandestine meeting in a Cocoa Beach, Florida, bungalow. Their mission was to develop a newspaper for the growing segment of the American population who no longer read newspapers. On Wednesday, 15 September 1982, the first multicolored, graphic-laden edition of *USA Today* rolled off the presses into Baltimore news racks resembling nineteen-inch televisions. The paper's national focus and penchant for tightly written, easily digested stories made it an instant sell-out. Two months later, *USA Today* already doubled Gannett's year-end projections (Farhi 12). More than two decades later, much of the skepticism that drove critics to label it "McPaper" has been replaced by general, if sometimes grudging, admiration. While its use of colorful graphics quickly became, and still remains, a driving design force in newspapers across the country, an increased emphasis on in-depth reporting earned it finalist status in the 2002 Pulitzer Prize competition (Pulitzer par. 10). More than two decades ago, the nation's largest newspaper publisher recognized an uncertain future unless sagging readership rebounded. Presently, *USA Today* boasts more than 2.3 million readers with a median age of forty-two, making it the most widely read daily in the country (Gannett par. 22).

The New York Times. Arthur Sulzberger, Jr., chair of the New York Times Company and publisher of its flagship newspaper, readily admits the critical need to redefine his industry. With Sulzberger at the helm, the New York Times is determined to remain not only one of the nation's leading newspapers, but also to become one of America's leading information sources as it develops multiple media platforms including print, cable television, and digital media. "Newspapers cannot be defined by the second word–paper. They've got to be defined by the first–news," he observes (Gates par. 12). In the newsrooms of the future, Sulzberg contends that reporters will develop their stories for a variety of media formats. No longer will the emphasis only be upon words, but also on still pictures and moving images. Thanks to the rise of these technologies, material developed for any single format can be adapted for other media forms as well. Information must span wider formats than has been the case in the past. For Sulzberg, these transitions must be targeted across the age spectrum and are broader than any single demographic.

Television Media

The television industry is continually reinventing itself in ongoing attempts to capture larger portions of the market. At times, these transformations have called even tried-and-true divisions within the industry to adapt. The lessons learned from these examples may serve as examples for the Church and preachers in particular.

The Tonight Show with Jay Leno. On Friday, 22 May 1992, a record audience tuned in to see Johnny Carson, the undisputed king of late night, stroll onstage through his billowing multicolored curtain for the last time. It was the end of an era in broadcast television. Months before, the network snubbed David Letterman as Carson's replacement, giving the nod to Jay Leno instead. The following Monday, *The Tonight Show with Jay Leno* aired for the very first time. When the new host strolled onto the star that marked his predecessor's place on stage, the set had been updated to some degree and a new band and musical score were in place, but little else had changed. In the year that followed since stepping onto Carson's stage, Leno's ratings tumbled. Critics doubted the new host's ability to resuscitate the late night program ("Leading" 1).

Leno wrestled with his producers for creative control of the show. By early 1995, he finally convinced NBC's executives and gained approval to shed himself of Carson's mantle. Like David the biblical shepherd boy preparing for battle with Goliath, Leno contended that he did not fit in Carson's armor. Instead, Leno opted for a much more intimate studio environment reminiscent of the comedy circuit he ruled prior to hosting the crown jewel of NBC's late night line-up. Carson's wide stage and billowing curtains were gone, replaced now with a shallow platform flanked by a video wall that Leno uses nightly to replay humorous clips from the news or take to the streets in one of his infamous "Jaywalking" features. The host eliminated the moat of empty space that once existed between Carson and his audience; today Leno literally walks into the arms of his adoring fans. Leno describes the transformation to PBS's Charlie Rose:

> People used to say, you know, "I listen to your monologue every night." And I said to myself, "You know, everyone's saying they listen to it. It's not radio. You're supposed to watch it." And I said, "You know, we need to give people something to watch, so let's put

some drop-ins in. Let's show Dole falling off the platform and put a funny cap around it." You know, let's say, "Folks, do you see this—take a look at this piece of footage," cut to something happening, then come back with a joke about it, so people had to watch the set. ("Leading" 12)

Despite the fact that Leno's changes expanded his market share of the coveted younger late night television advertising demographic, literally millions of Baby Boomers, Builders, and Seniors still tune in to watch his show.

NBC Nightly News with Tom Brokaw. In recent decades, the advent of cable news brought increasing competition to network television, resulting in a shift in the job description of the television news anchor. Rather than serving only as "talking heads" dispensing their stories from behind a desk, today's news anchors are becoming guides in an interactive news dialogue. Today Tom Brokaw routinely moves away from his news desk and stands with notes in hand before a large video wall where the day's stories come to life behind him. Interactivity is on the rise as producers tie television viewing with Internet usage. Michael Bartlett of the *USC Annenberg Online Journalism Review* looks at the future of news:

> NBC and MSNBC are experimenting with different ways to get viewers to turn into surfers: Nearly every evening on *NBC Nightly News*, anchor Tom Brokaw invites viewers to go to MSNBC to vote in a poll or get more information. The network does the same thing with *Dateline*. (par. 34)

Nightly News is mainstream network television, not MTV fare. Nevertheless, producers recognize the value of interacting with their viewers, regardless of age.

Purpose

The purpose of the study was to determine which factors relate to the use of visual media in preaching.

Research Questions

The following research questions provided the framework for this dissertation.

Research Question #1

How open or closed to change are survey respondents based on their responses to the Modified Rokeach E?

Research Question #2

To what degree are survey respondents either modern or postmodern in their orientation to culture?

Research Question #3

How receptive are survey respondents to the use of visual media in preaching?

Research Question #4

To what extent are respondents postliterate, and how does postliteracy relate to their receptivity to the use of visual media in preaching?

Research Question #5

What other variables might correlate with participant responses to the use of visual media in preaching?

Definition of Terms

The following terms are used throughout the project. The working definitions indicate how they are understood in the context of this study.

Preaching

The task of preaching is about helping people hear from God. At its most basic level, it involves a message, a messenger, and a recipient, all in the context of worship. Preaching never occurs in a vacuum; it always takes place within the contexts of Scripture and the lives of both the preacher and those in worship. Given this dynamic interplay, Phillips Brooks offers a classic definition of preaching as "the presentation of truth through personality" (5). While foundational, Brooks's eighteenth-century definition fails to recognize more recent developments, such as embracing a return to the ancient use of images in preaching. David Buttrick frames the cultural landscape of spiritual development in visual terms, observing that "Faith is formed in a nexus of image, symbol, metaphor, and ritual. Therefore, the language of preaching is essentially metaphorical" (125). Metaphor, icon, and image have long been the language of culture. For this study, preaching is defined as the cultural presentation of biblical truth through multifaceted means.

Dogmatism

In this study, dogmatism refers not to a set of beliefs nearly so much as to describe a person's natural openness or closedness to change. This dissertation adopts a working definition developed by Milton Rokeach in which he assesses a person's general intolerance, or dogmatism. Rather than examining the specific content of a person's beliefs, Rokeach's dogmatism studies seek to measure a person's general belief system.

Electronic Media

Grammatically, media is the plural form of the singular "medium," which generally refers to any method of mass communication such as newspaper, magazines, telephone, radio, television, or the Internet. Electronic media specifically refers to those forms of media that are encoded as electronic signals, transmitted, and then decoded. Joshua Meyrowitz expands the context for media in this way: "Media are many things at once: technologies, cultural artifacts, personal possessions, vessels for storing and retrieving cultural content and forms, and political and economic tools" (331). He adds that media do not grow in a vacuum, observing that "The growth of certain technologies and the particular uses and configurations of those technologies are stimulated by various social, political, and economic forces" (Meyrowitz 331).

This dynamic interplay between media forms and cultural forces has the capacity for reorganizing human thinking. In his foundational work titled *Understanding Media*, Marshall McLuhan first brought attention to his now famous dictum, "The medium is the message":

> In a culture like ours, long accustomed to splitting and dividing all things as a means of control, it is sometimes a bit of a shock to be reminded that, in operational and practical fact, the medium is the message. This is merely to say that the personal and social consequences of any medium—that is, of any extension of ourselves—result from the new scale that is introduced into our affairs by each extension of ourselves, or by any new technology. (23).

In this context, McLuhan contends that viewers become what they behold. People are influenced far more by various forms of media than they are by the content of their communication itself. In the same way that a book extends the reader's eye, McLuhan argues that electronic media extend the human central nervous system, giving the world an eye for an ear, so to speak. Richard Jensen expands on McLuhan's hypothesis:

> Marshall McLuhan taught us that the medium is not only the message; the medium is also the massage. McLuhan believed that the way we receive information (the message) is as important as the message itself. In an oral-aural world it is the ear that is massaged. (18)

Four decades after its release, McLuhan's hypothesis has been italicized by the ever-increasing speed and ever-expanding network of global electronic communications that massage the human senses. Thanks to the advent of cable television and the Internet, in particular, this phenomenon radically changes one's relation to space and time by compressing them twenty-four hours a day within a screen at arm's length.

Across two millennia, Christian history reveals that the spread of the gospel has been directly tied to its convergence with different forms of technology. World history reveals that humanity has experienced three eras of communication: oral, written, and now electronic. Today people live on the forefront of the shift from the second to third era of communication. Prior to these present times, human civilization has only shifted its dominant communications media once, and that alteration reformed most of the world as it existed up until that time. McLuhan observes that "the 16th century Renaissance was an age on the frontier between 2,000 years of alphabetic and manuscript culture, on the one hand, and the new mechanism of repeatability and quantification, on the other" (*Gutenberg* 173). Today much of the second shift from print to electronic communication puts the world between the now and not-yet; even worse, many pastors and laypeople hardly seem to be aware of the enormity of change that is at hand. Nevertheless, the Church must not lose heart, for Christian history records an uncanny ability by Jesus' followers to communicate his gospel in creative, compelling, and contemporary ways. Perhaps the Christian faith does not need to depend nearly so much on modern literate discourse to communicate its message. Despite the revolutionary shifts taking place today, the Christian Church is wise to recognize its remarkable ability to adapt to other media forms.

The Roman Road, for example, became the technological means by which the Apostle Paul and other early missionaries infiltrated Caesar's empire with the message of Jesus' life, ministry, crucifixion, and resurrection. In the Middle Ages, Martin Luther utilized the innovative technology of Gutenberg's press to promulgate his message to the masses. I am convinced that the Church can learn to proclaim the gospel in this new communication age as well. With that in mind, this study focused on electronic media as the use of video and digital graphics in conjunction with preaching.

Iconism and Aniconism

The Greek noun *eikon* is the origin of the English word "icon" and its biblical synonym often translated "image." Iconism is the position held by those in Church history who supported the use of visual media in worship while aniconism describe es the opposing view. Those who embraced the aniconic view were often called iconoclasts because many were literally "image-breakers" who not only opposed the use of visual imagery but were also known for making their case by decimating much of the Church's religious art and architecture.

Modernism and Modernity

The Renaissance, with its emphasis on the human being as the center of reality, gave birth to the Enlightenment and the modern era that extended well into the twentieth century. Its emphasis on humanity's utmost confidence in reason, rationality, and the rejection of the supernatural resulted in a mind-set that presumed human autonomy from divine restrictions. Michael Slaughter describes the anthropocentric focus of modernism:

> Modernity is a term that goes by other labels: the Age of Enlightenment or the Age of Reason. The basic premise of modernity is that all truth has its basis in matter and can be determined or measured by the scientific method, which uses the five senses (taste, touch, smell, hearing, and sight) to test hypotheses about causes and effects. If an idea or hypothesis can't be proven by science, then it is not "true." (31)

Leonard Sweet, Brian McLaren, and Jerry Haselmayer allude to Martin Luther's "Here I Stand" defense at the Diet of Worms in 1521 as a fitting mnemonic for understanding the essentials of modernity:

> *Here* = *Present:* Modernity focused on the here and now. It

understood itself as having moved beyond the past–the Roman Catholic medieval past; the past that trusted authorities, the past that revered kings as ruling by divine right, the past that understood the earth to be the center of the universe.

I = Individualism: Descartes' later dictum "I think therefore I am" doubled the emphasis on "I"–the individual thinker, the individual knower, the autonomous individual increasingly disconnected from both the human community and the Creator.

Stand = Static Propositions and Stable Physical Laws: The modern world was confident that, just as there were discernable laws that governed the physical universe, there were free-floating moral laws and spiritual standards upon which one could stand in certainty. (199-200)

This study considers modernism a worldview that embraces reason, objective truth, human freedom, and inevitable progress. By the same token, modernity can be understood as the historical era when this outlook reigned supreme.

Postmodernism and Postmodernity

By contrast, postmodernism is literally defined as that which follows the modern age, with its confidence in progress and knowledge. Postmodern culture does not strictly find its meaning in antithetical terms, however. In this case, "postmodern" should not be mistaken as strictly "non-modern" or even "anti-modern," but seen as that which not only comes after modernism but also through it. Sweet, McLaren, and Haselmayer speak to those who are familiar with the Hegelian dialectic:

> It may be tempting to see modernity as the thesis and postmodernity as the antithesis. We believe a better approach would be to see premodernity as the thesis, modernity as the antithesis, and postmodernity as an attempt at synthesis–an attempt that is still in its earliest stages (242).

Chuck Smith, Jr. views this emerging age as more disjointed:

> Postmodernity combines "the old and the new," not in an attempt to produce a "wonderful blend" but rather in a playful irony that tends to flatten the chain of command, undermine power structures, and invent new realities. Unlike modernity, postmodernity rejects the integrity of a single style. (*End* 46)

This emerging philosophy, which can be traced in part through the twentieth century thinking of Jacques Derrida, Michel Foucault, and Jean-François Lyotard, emphasizes a tolerance for ambiguity. Lyotard is renowned for his succinct definition of the term in his now classic text *The Postmodern Condition: A Report on Knowledge*, in which he states, "Simplifying to the extreme, I define postmodern as incredulity toward metanarratives" (xxiv). By metanarratives, Lyotard refers to the universal truths proliferated within a culture that are ultimately used to legitimate a particular worldview, perspective, or value system (Williams 32). Instead, Lyotard extols "parology," which is a deliberate disregard for conventional norms of thinking (Cahoone 269-270). Foucault determines that so-called "truth" depends largely upon the assumptions of the age in which it is developed (Strathern 22-23). Likewise, Derrida questions the ability of philosophy to operate on its own terms. Thomas Jay Oord describes the way postmodernism unravels modern thinking:

> As interpretation and reinterpretation occurs, the reader comes to realize that no foundational, final, or fixed interpretation is available. Words refer to other words, those refer to other words, and those refer to still others; the process has no end. Meaning is found in matrices, but these matrices are finally groundless. The practice of grammatology reveals the emptiness of logocentrism by deconstructing all concepts or norms tied to a center. (1)

Derrida calls this process of identifying the assumptions of truth in any given field "deconstruction." Critics would be mistaken to caricature postmoderns as irrational, however. Instead, they question the ability of human reason to hold objectively all the answers to life's questions. Tom Beaudoin confesses, "Xers make great heretics" (121).

However, critics of postmodernism should not mistakenly believe that this emerging worldview is wholly opposed to the Judeo-Christian ethic. The postmodern emphasis on holism is much more closely akin to the biblical worldview than much of the atomistic ideology of the modern age. Likewise, postmodern ecological concerns connect with the Christian's call to stewardship of the earth. Postmoderns emphasize the organic over the mechanistic, the whole rather than the part, networks over organizations, collaboration over competition, and the spiritual over the scientific. Slaughter finds his lowest common denominator in this final description of postmodernism, stating that *"post-modern* means *post-scientific.* I do not mean the rejection of the scientific method, but the rejection of the premise that all truth can be defined only by science, by the five empirical senses" (31). Smith expands his definition, saying that postmodernism not only comes after scientism, it also comes after rationalism, historicism, absolutism, realism, ethnocentrism, and objectivism (*End* 47-86). In this emerging postmodern age, the challenge is to begin with the message of the gospel birthed in premodernity, coupled with the reasons developed in modernity, to supply the kind of signs and symbols that will lead postmoderns to an authentic experience of God and his truth.

Stanley Grenz differentiates postmodernism from postmodernity in his *Primer on Postmodernism*:

> *Postmodernism* [original emphasis] refers to an intellectual mood and an array of cultural expressions that call into question the ideals, principles, and values that lay at the heart of the modern mind-set. *Postmodernity* [original emphasis], in turn, refers to an emerging epoch, the era in which we are living, the time when the postmodern outlook increasingly shapes our society. Postmodernity is the era in which postmodern ideas, attitudes, and values reign–when postmodernism molds culture. It is the era of the postmodern society. (12)

While not specifically addressing postmodernity by name, Buttrick frames the preacher's challenge in this emerging age in his classic text *Homiletic*:

> We live in mysteries and we are a mystery to ourselves. Not only are there huge questions connected with being human–Why are we here on a whirling ball of earth? Why are we born and why do we die?–but there are also mysteries within the human self. In spite of our psychoanalytic wisdoms, we do not know ourselves. We may paste name tags on our souls, or trace genealogies, but we cannot answer the question of identity. We sense that, through all our days and years, we are being formed so that, at any given moment, we cannot say exactly who we are. Even our motives defy analysis: The fabric of impulse, desire, dream, and pretension is too thickly woven within us to follow separate strands. Besides, when we do look at ourselves and, indeed, into ourselves, we always catch ourselves posing! The self is a conundrum. Moreover, the human enterprise itself defies understanding. Every day, like a shaken kaleidoscope, the human world patterns differently in consciousness. We can scan headlines or peruse chapters in history, but, unfinished, the human story is uncertain. In sum, human being in the world is mysterious. We make meaning with metaphor by bumping mysteries together. The only

way we have access to our own depth is by metaphor. (121)

In the modern age, preaching was effective because it adapted itself to the communication styles of the culture. Preaching in the postmodern age will be effective as preachers understand the time and culture of this emerging age and faithfully communicate the timeless message of Scripture, even to people who reject the rigidities of modernistic rationalism, embrace the supernatural, and resist the modern urge to be categorized. For preachers, this new understanding will require the retooling of their homiletical instruments beyond words and sentences only to also include metaphor and image as well. This study defines postmodernism as the presently emerging ideology following the modern age that questions human ability to reason and rule objectively. Postmodernity is defined as the age in which this thought finds expression.

Literacy

In the modern age, and in most circles yet today, literacy is narrowly understood as the ability to read written language. This study, in conjunction with the work of literacy researchers, recognizes gradations across the spectrum of literacy. Today relatively few adults in the United States are truly illiterate. By the same token, a considerable number of adults with low literacy skills lack the foundation they need to find and keep decent jobs, support their children's education, and participate actively in civic life. This broader understanding of literacy recognizes the importance of being able to perform across a wide array of tasks that reflect the types of materials and demands people encounter in their daily lives. As a result, the Adult Education and Family Literacy Act of 1998 defines literacy as "an individual's ability to read, write, speak in English, compute and solve problems at levels of proficiency necessary to function on the job, in the family of the individual and in society" (1061).

David Smith cautions against such modern interpretations of literacy, however. He observes that "it might be best to define reading not in terms of a set of skills one possesses but rather as a social practice confined within a particular cultural context" (30). He goes on to note that in many cultures, people could be considered illiterate, not because they were unable to communicate the language of everyday life but because they lacked fluency in a particularly esteemed language such as Latin. This study recognizes the need for a broader view regarding literacy, embracing Smith's caution to Western minds that "it is difficult to avoid the assumption that literary skills are an essential ingredient in daily experience" (25). In Chapter 2, this project examines literacy forms more fully, both in Scripture and in contemporary life today.

Postliteracy

In light of the broader understanding of literacy advocated above, postliteracy is a term I originally uncovered in Len Wilson's unpublished graduate thesis at United Theological Seminary and further defined to describe individuals who are able to read and write but who choose to gain access to information by means other than linear forms like the printed page. Late in the literature review, I found the term postliteracy used in Jensen's subtitle: *Thinking in Story: Preaching in a Post-Literate Age*, in which he observes that "the preacher in an oral culture thinks in stories while the preacher in a literate culture thinks in ideas" (9). Tom Boomershine writes the foreword to Jensen's book, underscoring the transformation taking place between textual and visual media forms:

> In this electronic age, the church faces a new communications challenge: how is the gospel of Jesus Christ to be proclaimed and made meaningful in a culture that no longer values literacy and its modes of thought as the most advanced means of communication? This is the first period in the history of Christianity in which the most powerful medium of cultural communication is not writing. From a communications perspective, therefore, we live in the period of the greatest change since the formation of the church. (Foreword 13)

While not using the term specifically, Bill Easum defines the boundaries well with a challenging observation in the foreword to Len Wilson and Jason Moore's most recent book titled *Digital Storytellers*:

> A whole new digital world is emerging today. Can you see it? If you can, you know it is a world built on emotional, virtual, holographic, decentralized, holistic, empowered, one-to-one, borderless, bottom-up, global/local, and egalitarian characteristics. Such a world will play by totally different rules than the rules of modernity. In the twenty-first century to *not be digital* [original emphasis] will be the new form of illiteracy. (11)

My review of the literature found that Tony Schwarz, who was one of McLuhan's own students, is the first to introduce the term postliterate in 1981. He proposes a helpful definition of living in a postliterate age: "We have become a post-literate society. Electronic media rather than the printed word are now our major means of non-face-to-face communication" (11). In the same way that oral-aural communication massaged the ear, and writing and print communication massaged the eye, electronic communication simultaneously massages a variety of human senses. Jensen makes a case for 1985 being an important milepost in postliterate culture, observing that it "was the first year that more videocassettes were checked out/rented from video stores than there were books checked out of libraries. Many libraries, of course, have now become videobraries as well" (49).

Postliteracy recognizes a new set of relationships among earlier concepts. It refers to the degree to which people who are naturally capable of accessing print media now prefer nonlinear visual communication forms like video and the Internet as their primary sources of information instead.

Historical and Theological Foundations

The history of redemption in Scripture reveals God's passionate desire to communicate with creation. Without saying a word, God's created order is drawn to its Creator through nature and history, also called general revelation. The psalmist describes this theological tenet in poetic terms in Psalm 19:1-4a:

> The heavens declare the glory of God; the skies proclaim the work of his hands. Day after day they pour forth speech; night after night they display knowledge. There is no speech or language where their voice is not heard. Their voice goes out into all the earth, their words to the ends of the world.

In the New Testament, the Apostle Paul expounds further in Romans 1:20: "Ever since the creation of the world his eternal power and divine nature, indivisible though they are, have been understood and seen through the things he has made. So they are without excuse."

Scripture also testifies that God has not limited himself to general revelation as his only means of connection. Special revelation refers to God's redemptive purpose manifested specifically in the person of Jesus Christ. Furthermore, the pages of both testaments point to the Messiah's personal fulfillment of salvation history. The writer of the book of Hebrews begins with this observation:

> In the past God spoke to our forefathers through the prophets at many times and in various ways, but in these last days he has spoken

to us by his Son, whom he appointed heir of all things, and through whom he made the universe. The Son is the radiance of God's glory and the exact representation of his being, sustaining all things by his powerful word. (Heb. 1:1-3a)

Scripture makes it clear that this passion to communicate with humanity flows from the heart of God himself.

The aural world of biblical times depended on an oral storytelling tradition. Over time, faith community leaders fixated on written language and made the shift to textual forms. This transition resulted in the establishment of the Canon and an educated, literate clergy who ministered to a vastly illiterate, premodern constituency.

Evangelicalism has long held the printed words of Scripture in high regard. Coupled with its aim of connecting people to God, the evangelical Church grew out of Martin Luther's call to *sola scriptura* by placing its emphasis on Scripture over other hermeneutical sources, including the traditions of the Church. Likewise, John Wesley is well known for his passionate desire to be *homo unius libri*, a man of one book: the Holy Bible. Fueled by the modern era's power of the press, the Protestant Reformation became a "Religion of the Book," and over time a textual bias that presupposed the literacy of its people branded evangelical preaching. Authority centered on written rather than spoken words. As the laity became increasingly literate over the centuries that followed, emphasis shifted from a concern for the efficaciousness of Scripture, centering instead on its exactness, resulting in the Church's long-fought arguments over biblical inerrancy in recent decades.

Gutenberg's press gave rise to the first mass medium, which brought literacy to the uneducated and changed the way people structured their religious, not to mention cultural, interactions. As it shifted from an emphasis on the centralized traditions of the Church and its liturgies to Scriptures that were increasingly accessible, the Bible became a centerpiece of Protestant worship. Over time, Western culture became print driven as common people learned to read primarily through a process of textual biblical education. Jensen describes the effect of this transformation on preaching: "Gutenberg hermeneutics . . . created Gutenberg homiletics. Gutenberg homiletics . . . predisposes a didactic form of homiletics (7). In many ways, history validates Jensen's thesis, showing that the advent of modernism found its way into the world through the Church. Lesslie Newbigin, former bishop of the Church of South India, observes that "[w]ith hindsight, it is now easy to see how many of the self-evident truths of the Enlightenment were self-evident only to those who were the heirs of a thousand years of Christian teaching" (48). Today, the world is in flux once more with the emergence of postmodernism, but this time, the roles are reversed and the Church is late in encountering it. Michael Polanyi, the Hungarian chemist and philosopher, observes the Church's marriage to modern thought this way: "Its incandescence has fed on the combustion of the Christian heritage in the oxygen of Greek rationalism, and when the fuel was exhausted the critical framework burned away" (265).

Thomas Troeger describes two innovations that accompanied the modern homiletic: the first came as the authority of biblical interpretation shifted from the clergy to the people; the second came with the translation of Scripture into the vernacular (13). This technical innovation led to the mass production of the Bible via the printing press. D. T. Max observes that the power of the press "replaced the hand-copied manuscript with a bloodless mass-produced object, the book" (20). Pierre Babin and Mercedes Iannone concur, quoting Richard Molard from *Horizons protestants*, which is now out of print:

> Protestantism was born with printing and has been the religion in which printing—the printed Bible, the catechism, newspapers, and journals—has played a vital part. The present crisis in these publications is undoubtedly a sign of a very deep crisis of identity. How is it possible to be a Protestant in a world in which radio and television are the easiest forms of communication? (25)

The Church's challenge in this emerging era is not to embrace a postmodern worldview necessarily, but to discover new ways of conveying the message of Scripture to postmodern people of all ages in an increasingly visual, electronic culture.

Generational Distinctives

Popular folklore says that a frog placed in a kettle of boiling water will instinctively jump out of its deadly environment. By the same token, frogs that are placed in cool water can be boiled alive if the heat is gradually increased because frogs are unable to differentiate incremental changes in their environment. Following this analogy, human beings often find it difficult to identify cultural changes with much precision when they creep incrementally into their lives. Today, preachers face the challenge of assessing the impact of cultural shifts such as postmodernism while they are in the midst of the transition. In spite of these challenges, social scientists and demographers have studied changes in birth rates and particular generational experiences like the end of World War II or the introduction of the birth control pill to differentiate demographic groups. Generally, they stratify America's twentieth-century generations into five groups (see Table 1).

Table 1. Twentieth Century Generations in the United States

Generational Names	Birth Years
Seniors	Before 1925
Builders	Between 1925-44
Baby Boomers	Between 1945-63
Baby Busters or Generation X	1964-80
Millenialists	After 1980

Beneath these generational distinctions flows another cultural current related to media forms and the rise of technology:

> [T]he twentieth century was about the gestation, birth, and development of a new era, with its own particular communications system. Different people cite different birth dates, from 1896's film to 1927's film with sound to the 1949-1950 TV "revolution" to 1962's color TV "revolution" to 1968's social "revolution." Historians will clarify these discussions. What matters is that we are now a few generations into a new culture, and the watershed moment, somewhere across our postmodern landscape, has already occurred. The digital deconstruction has been happening for years now, and only the most unplugged churches are unaware of the upheaval. (Wilson and Moore 14)

Clearly the impact of both postmodernism and electronic media forms is most evident among Baby Busters since they are the first generation of adults to live entirely in their wake. For them, the cultural kettle seems unchanged because they have known no other world. By the same token, Seniors, Builders, and Baby Boomers have also been affected by these cultural changes and have in varying degrees adapted to life in this emerging time kettle as evidenced from popular opinion polls and the fact that habitual television viewers can be found in every demographic stratum. Likewise, the use of the Internet continues to grow exponentially across the age spectrum.

While many observe today that Baby Busters and Millenialists often come from "nontraditional" homes and yearn for the kind of meaningful relationships they lacked in childhood, a good number of these same cultural issues can characterize displaced Seniors and Builders to varying degrees as well. Although these older individuals likely grew up in a much more traditional culture, they often share much more in common with their younger descendants than many realize since many of them also know how it feels to yearn for similar kinds of personal connections to fill the void left in their lives. In their case, however, the loss may be attributed to the death of a spouse, the relocation of grown children to other regions of the country, or the loss of a home in order to receive higher levels of personal care. Regardless, both age groups share similar experiences in the end despite their age or upbringing. John Reid, Lesslie Newbigin, and David Pullinger describe how the emerging postmodern age affects more than just the youngest generations:

> Christians, like others, rarely contain just one framework for living—in us are postmodernism, modernism and traditional or pre-modern elements. In this way we share the lack of integration, and fragmentation, that mark this period. Postmodernism and modernism come to us through culture. (46-47)

Context of the Project

New Hope Community Church of the Nazarene launched its first public service on 23 October 1988. Founded by Pastor Tom Wilson, the church employed methods taught by the church growth movement at that time. More specifically, New Hope Community Church modeled itself after Willow Creek Community Church in South Barrington, Illinois, Saddleback Community Church in Lake Forest, California, and Dale Galloway's church in Portland, Oregon, from which Pastor Wilson borrowed the name.

Originally planted in the seeker-sensitive tradition as a church for the unchurched, New Hope rapidly became the fastest growing church plant in the Church of the Nazarene. Launched on the Tempe-Chandler border in the southeast valley of the Phoenix metroplex, the rapidly growing community was ripe with opportunities for a church intent on sharing Christ in creative, compelling ways. From the outset, the church was fortunate to be able to lease a new state-of-the-art high school auditorium in the epicenter of new housing and commercial development. By 1992, Easter Sunday attendance swelled to nearly nine hundred.

In the years that followed, the church continued to grow, averaging nearly five hundred men, women, and children each week. However, everything changed on Sunday, 1 September 1996 when Pastor Wilson suddenly resigned after a bitter dispute with leadership. At the conclusion of his sermon, Pastor Wilson reached into his jacket pocket and read his resignation letter to the congregation without any prior knowledge of the board or district superintendent. He concluded by saying, "This is my last Sunday," and walked off the stage to the shock of everyone. The pastor's abrupt resignation resulted in the immediate loss of over two hundred people the following week. These losses were never regained, and the hemorrhage continued for nearly three long years. As is often the case with pastors who follow winsome predecessors, Wilson's successor was seemingly doomed from the outset. He left the ministry entirely after two years of intense personal and professional difficulty at the helm. By June 1999, New Hope was officially declared a "church in crisis" by the district superintendent, making it eligible for denominational assistance. I was appointed New Hope's third pastor with fifty men, women, and children remaining in attendance. By this time, the church met in an old elementary school lunchroom rather than the spacious accoutrements the church had known previously. For many people, New Hope had literally become "No Hope Church."

During my interview with the board at New Hope, I discovered that Pastor Wilson, a talented preacher and gifted sketch artist, often drew large format cartoons as he preached. By the conclusion of his sermon, the completed artwork bolstered his theme. I learned that his method was particularly popular during the image-rich seasons of Christmas and Easter. This discovery set the groundwork for my own interest in using electronic visual media in my preaching.

After much prayer, my family and I believed God called us to lead New Hope into its next chapter of ministry. My training at the feet of Dr. Dale Galloway and exposure to leading-edge churches around the world fit well with New

Hope's core values. My own interests in preaching with visual media appeared to be the digital offspring or next generation of Pastor Wilson's model. With fear and trembling, my family and I moved to Phoenix in hopes of seeing New Hope rise from its "No Hope" ashes.

Description of the Project

As shown in Appendix A, the project consisted of a researcher-designed, cross-sectional quantitative survey of attitudes toward the use of visual media in preaching. The survey employed a number of researcher-designed questions coupled with congregational responses to a short form of the Rokeach Dogmatism Scale (E) and questions adapted from two nonstandardized surveys of postmodernism. The first source, called the Postmodern Identification Questionnaire (see Appendix B), was developed by Dan Huckins for his doctor of ministry dissertation at Asbury Theological Seminary in 1998. It was utilized as a research instrument in Paul Clines' Asbury dissertation in 1999. Les Steele and Bob Drovdahl formulated their Postmodernism Survey for informational use with their students at Seattle Pacific University (see Appendix C). This nonstandardized survey was also revised by Stanley Grenz from Carey Theological College in Vancouver, British Columbia. Mark Gooden utilized it in his 2003 dissertation at Asbury. Prior to their use in this project, written permission to use material from these surveys was granted by all four individuals provided that appropriate citations of the original sources were made.

On Sunday, 21 September 2003, subjects were encouraged to remain after the morning worship encounter to complete the survey. Confidentiality was ensured by encouraging respondents not to place any identifying information on the survey apart from specific demographic material requested. Five adolescents, aged 14 to 17, completed the survey; parents for these minors signed a Parental Consent Form (see Appendix D). Upon completion, respondents placed their anonymous surveys in the church's offering basket. A number of parishioners who were not in attendance on the primary day of data collection turned in their surveys in the ten-day period that followed.

Methodology

This dissertation was a correlational study examining the relationship between congregational assessments regarding the use of visual media in preaching and respondents' dogmatism and personal orientations toward postmodernism. The research project was an evaluative study in the nonexperimental mode utilizing a researcher-designed quantitative cross-sectional survey that incorporated a standardized dogmatism scale. No comparison group was used to evaluate the use of visual media in preaching at New Hope. Given the fact that I had been using visual media in my preaching at the church for over four years already, a cross-sectional design was necessary since a baseline was no longer available.

Variables

Since this study was done in the nonexperimental mode, there were no dependent, independent, or intervening variables as are used in an experimental study. Instead, this study examined the relationships between a number of variables including the degree to which respondents were dogmatic, their receptivity to the use of visual media in preaching, and the degrees to which respondents viewed themselves as both postmodern and postliterate. Other variables that might affect the outcome of the study were age, gender, church experience, church affiliation, and tenure at New Hope. Since the study utilized a cross-sectional survey, the treatment varied by respondent depending upon that person's tenure at New Hope.

Instrumentation and Data Collection

In consultation with Dr. William Brown, who is a professor of organizational psychology at Arizona State University and also a member of my research and reflection team, I designed the questionnaire to correlate congregational receptivity to visual media in preaching with dogmatism, postmodernism, and postliteracy. The Modified Rokeach E, a widely tested standardized scale developed in 1960, was used to measure dogmatism, or a respondent's natural receptivity to change. In addition to this scale, attitudes toward the use of visual media in preaching were explored through a number of researcher-designed questions. Finally, respondent attitudes toward postmodern culture were assessed by including some nonstandardized survey elements from the Huckins and Steele-Drovdahl-Grenz questionnaires (see Appendixes B and C), as well as several more researcher-designed questions. Five members of the research and reflection team volunteered to pretest the instrument on Sunday, 24 August 2003.

Delimitations and Generalizability

By definition, postmodernism is often best understood by what it is not: it does not subscribe to the conventions of the modern age with its reliance upon the scientific method to validate human existence. Postmodernism is an emerging era, making clear delineations very difficult. The world is at a hinge point in history, an in-between time. As such, postmoderns are likewise very difficult to define. Many researchers, following modern constructs, equate their definitions of postmodernism with a specific age group (e.g., Baby Busters) as outlined earlier in the chapter. Yet one of the identifying characteristics of postmodern people tends to be their natural disinclination to be categorized or swallowed up by sweeping generalizations. Calvin Miller observes that "the arrival of the postmodern mind-set has presented a particularly difficult challenge. Postmoderns have accepted their category while denying they can be categorized" (Foreword 9). This project presumes that postmodernism is not only generationally related but also becoming more culturally pervasive across the age spectrum. In other words, postmodernism is emerging as a cultural mind-set that is shaping not only Baby Busters and Millenialists but people of all ages to varying degrees.

By the same token, the generalizations of this study will be increasingly hopeful to pastors as the postmodern era continues to emerge, particularly for those who serve in intergenerational settings. Given the cross-sectional context for this study after four years of treatment, it would be a mistake to presume that the inclusion of visual media in preaching would produce immediate results in a congregation which was not accustomed to its use. The findings from this study can only be generalized by other congregations to the degree they are similar to New Hope. However, the findings offer hope for those who desire to engage intergenerational congregations visually. This study seeks to identify correlations between dogmatism, postliteracy, and postmodernism in relation to a person's receptivity toward the use of visual media in preaching.

Population

The subject population included all attenders of New Hope, age 14 and older, regardless of membership status. The subjects were self-selected volunteers. Data were gathered from subjects once in a single setting with a cross-sectional survey. Prior to the administration of the survey, public announcements were made to explain the project and solicit the broadest congregational participation possible. Since the research design involved the use of a cross-sectional survey, a posttest was not administered.

Importance

The impetus for this study grew out of my surprise over the broad demographic New Hope's ministry model was drawing. As a pastor, and drawing on my experiences in the Beeson program, I suspected that the use of visual media in preaching and worship would attract a younger demographic primarily. Instead, New Hope has drawn people of all ages, including a good number of older people outside their target demographic. This study takes seriously the preaching task and seeks to test whether or not the use of visual media in preaching connects better with those in a particular age demographic or with people of various ages who see themselves as predominantly postmodern and/or postliterate.

Overview of the Dissertation

In Chapter 2, my literature review establishes the biblical, theological, and homiletical context for the study. This theoretical framework includes a survey of postmodernism, including its philosophical parameters and its practical impact on the Church today. Chapter 3 provides a more detailed explanation of the design of the study. Chapter 4 furnishes an analysis of the survey findings while Chapter 5 reports the major findings of the study and offers suggestions for further inquiry.

CHAPTER TWO

PRECEDENTS IN THE LITERATURE

The human creation is complex, consisting of individuals who interact with each other and the world through a full menu of communication forms. The Bible is replete with examples of God's multichanneled outreach to creation as revealed through the human senses of sight (Isa.6:10; Matt. 6:26), smell (Job 27:3; 1 Cor. 12:17), sound (Gen. 4:10; Isa. 6:10; Matt. 11:15), touch (Ps. 144:5; 1 John 1:1), and taste (Ps. 34:8; Matt. 5:13). In his ministry, Jesus used a wide variety of learning experiences to convey his message: he washed his disciples' feet, held up a little child before them as an example, broke bread before them, used coins and withered trees for object lessons, and at one point even wrote in the dirt to make his point. For centuries, the Church of Jesus Christ embraced worship as the reverent celebration of God's redeemed people through a variety of forms that connected with the human senses through flickering flames, crusty fragments of bread, and the pungent aroma of incense. By the same token, the evangelical Church in particular has long betrayed a literary bias that elevates the written and spoken word nearly to the exclusion of all other communication modes. Robert Webber considers the ramifications of this bias, observing that too much "of our Protestant worship is suffering from verbal overdose" (*Worship Phenomenon* 88).

Evangelicals root themselves in the verbal and textual traditions. With the possible exception of a cross, few other visual symbols are typically displayed in most churches today. In their quest to be people of the Word, evangelicals have become people of words, excluding nearly every other form of communication in their preaching and worship. Following Jesus' analogy to the blind guides in Matthew 23:24, evangelicals run the risk of straining gnats and swallowing camels by having more concern for the exactness of the words of Scripture rather than the efficaciousness of the biblical teaching itself. As a result, George Barna observes that a good deal of ministry today is informational rather than transformational:

> At present the Church is intensely geared to pastors and other seminary-trained staff disseminating accurate and appropriate theological knowledge; . . . conveying Bible truths and related information in the same ways we have always done . . . will further hamper our potential to penetrate a changing society with God's timeless and priceless truths. (*Second* 57)

Throughout history, important shifts in human beliefs, lifestyles, values, and even styles of learning have been triggered by technological change. Martin Luther, for example, capitalized on the power of Gutenberg's press in his attacks against papal and ecclesiastical abuses. By communicating his message to the masses in their own language through the power of the printed page, Luther capitalized on a media revolution that ushered in the Protestant Reformation.

The half-life of today's technologies is unprecedented, and their impact is widespread and worldwide. Slaughter cites Wilson, noting that while 99.9 percent of Americans have televisions, only 97 percent have plumbing (23). Television is not only pervasive in America, but thanks to satellite technologies, it can be found in the farthest reaches of the globe. Even remote villages that are dependent upon generated electricity often have a satellite receiver dish somewhere on the compound. Furthermore, studies have shown that the effects of extended television viewing over time impacts the attention spans of those watching it.

Despite the technological opportunities available today, the Church must never compromise its mandate to relate God's love to the world through Jesus Christ. However, the media forms, strategies, and styles used must be flexible in communicating to an ever-changing culture. The challenge for the twenty-first-century preacher is to communicate the timeless message of the gospel in ways that penetrate the fluidity of culture while at the same time remaining grounded in the biblical and theological bedrock of the faith. Fortunately, two thousand years of Church history offer a rich soil of biblical and theological precedent for preachers who are intent on creatively engaging their culture.

Biblical and Theological Precedents

On many occasions Jesus utilized nonverbal methods in his communication of spiritual truth. His first-century forms of multimedia were admittedly not as sophisticated as the electronic tools available to churches today. Instead, they took the form of concrete, three-dimensional object lessons. Whether he challenged his disciples to demonstrate childlike faith or lifted a cup and broken loaf as emblems of his shed blood and broken body, Jesus reminds the Church in a myriad of ways that while faith comes by hearing, it also comes by seeing.

Old Testament Forms

The Hebrew Scriptures begin with these words in Genesis 1:1: "In the beginning God created the heavens and the earth." With this phrase, Scripture introduces its primary and most prolific image: not of a garden, or even the earth, but of God as Creator. This image of his artistic creation unfolds in Genesis through imagery that is as compelling today as it was to those who first heard it: light and darkness; land, sky, and sea; vegetation and animals, all culminating in human beings who are made in the image of the First Artist (Gen. 1:26).

The Old Testament is rich with vivid imagery. Following Genesis, the book of Exodus not only chronicles Israel's dramatic flight from Egypt but also details the construction of the Tabernacle and the Ark of the Covenant. In Exodus, Moses goes to extreme lengths in specifying construction details and the roles played by a wide variety of skilled artisans. For example, a member of the tribe of Judah named Bezalel is extolled in Exodus 35-36 for becoming what might be called the patron saint of artists. By his example, Bezalel demonstrates that followers of the First Artist can honor him not only with folded hands but also with hands that are creatively inspired by God to carve, or weave, or cut stone.

By the same token, critics of biblical imagery find strong footing in the book of Exodus, and more particularly the Decalogue itself, using it as their foundation for iconoclasm. At Mount Sinai, Moses received the Ten Commandments as outlined in Exodus 20:1-17. Critics contend that the second commandment is clear:

> You shall not make for yourself an idol in the form of anything in heaven above or on the earth beneath or in the waters below. You shall not bow down to them or worship them; for I, the LORD your God, am a jealous God, punishing the children for the sins of the fathers to the third and fourth generation of those who hate me, but showing love to a thousand generations of those who love me and keep my commandments.

By the same token, Bezalel's prominence among the Israelites as an example of God-inspired artisanship seems to differentiate the crafting of material idols from the use of artistic symbolism in Israelite worship. Likewise, Solomon brings Hiram from Tyre to fashion works of bronze in 1 Kings 7:14. Webber speaks directly to the handiwork of the Tabernacle artisans:

> These symbols belonged to the worship of Israel and were the context for a meeting between God and God's people–"there I will meet with you" (v. 22). These symbols were for a meeting between God and God's people... These symbols were not to exist outside of worship as art objects, but inside worship as the symbols of God's presence. Consequently, they became the essential link that expressed the meeting of Israel with God. (*Music* 488)

Properly understood, the elements of Israel's Tabernacle worship pointed to their invisible God without attempting to fashion his likeness into physical form. Bezalel, and countless other artisans, offered the work of their hands to point to the First Artist.

Even when God the First Artist uses words in the Old Testament, he often combines them with graphic imagery. The prophet Isaiah is a good case in point. In Isaiah 20, God instructs the prophet to strip off his clothes and walk around naked for three years. Through this extreme example, God wants to get his point across that Egypt is about to be carted off to Assyria, stripped and naked, along with anyone else who fails to place their trust in him. Likewise, one of the most profound object lessons in the Old Testament comes in the eighteenth chapter of Jeremiah's prophetic book. Here, God leads Jeremiah to a potter's house where he offers all of Israel a vivid object lesson through the artisan's work on the wheel. Only after the visual message is first communicated through the potter reforming his marred creation does God speaks to Jeremiah: "Like clay in the hand of the potter, so are you in my hand, O house of Israel" (Jer. 18:6b). In this example, words follow the primacy of imagery. Through both words and images, the Old Testament offers a full menu of multisensory forms to communicate vividly the First Artist's passionate desire to fulfill his redemptive purposes for human creation.

New Testament Forms

Ironically, the Gospel of John begins with reference to a word that is actually an image: "In the beginning was the Word, and the Word was with God, and the Word was God. He was with God in the beginning" (John 1:1-2). In this way, John introduces his gospel by affirming that Jesus is God in the flesh. Later in the New Testament, the Apostle Paul writes to the church at Colosse that Jesus "is the image of the invisible God" (Col. 1:15). The heart of the New Testament message is that a fleshed-out faith stands at the epicenter of Christianity, for as Leonid Ouspensky and Vladimir Lossky note, "Christianity is the revelation not only of the Word of God, but also of the

Image of God, in which His likeness is revealed" (27).

This understanding of God's image dwelling in human flesh is given the theological term Incarnation, literally meaning the "enfleshment" of God in human form. Webber asserts the supremacy of Christ:

> The greatest of all metaphors is Jesus. He is, as Paul said, 'the exact likeness of the unseen God.' He brings the invisible into visible form and his death and resurrection become the metaphors for our death to sin and our resurrection to new life in him. (*Younger* 69)

J. Kenneth Grider sets the term in theological context:

> Incarnation means that God was not content simply to think good thoughts about us, nor to help us while keeping a safe distance from us. It means that God visited us for our salvation–"in our sorry case," as the ancient Athanasius expressed it. (279)

In beautiful prose, Frederick Buechner introduces his now classic book *The Faces of Jesus* with this observation of Incarnation:

> *He had a face* [original emphasis]... Whoever he was or was not, whoever he thought he was, whoever he has become in the memories of men since and will go on becoming for as long as men remember him–exalted, sentimentalized, debunked, made and remade to the measure of each generation's desire, dread, indifference–he was a man once, whatever else he may have been. And he had a man's face, a human face. So suppose, as the old game goes, that we could return in time and see it for ourselves, see the face of Jesus as it actually was two thousand years of faces back. *Ecce homo*, Pilate said–*Behold the man* [original emphasis] – yet whatever our religion or lack of it, we tend to shrink from beholding him... But with Jesus the risk is too great; the risk that his face would be too much for us if not enough, either a face like any other face to see, pass by, forget, or a face so unlike any other that we would have no choice but to remember it always and follow or flee it to the end of our days and beyond. (9)

The plenary message of Scripture is that God Incarnate stepped down into the human predicament. He spoke a human language. He embraced human culture. Likewise, he also embraced human suffering, grief, sin, and guilt. Sweet speaks of the Incarnation in everyday language:

What if God had refused to dumb down? This is the essence of the Incarnation—God came to us. God's good ship "Grace" did not disdain shallow waters. God didn't stand against us, but walked alongside us. The heart of the Incarnation is God's willingness to communicate through kenosis (emptying) toward the goal of plerosis (filling). God's dumbing down was for our wising up. (*AquaChurch* 167)

The doctrine of the Incarnation underscores that creation is not beyond redemption and that the gospel always meets people where they are in the same moment it calls them to new life in Christ. This revelation comes through ordinary human language. As Millard Erickson asserts, "When God describes Himself in His revelation, He speaks of Himself not as He is in Himself, but as we conceive of Him" (52). Furthermore, the Incarnation also stands as an ongoing visible reminder that God sends Christians into the popular culture in a way not too far removed from the way he sent Jesus into the world. In the end, this Incarnational understanding of ministry should compel preachers to follow Paul's model in 1 Cor. 9:22: "To the weak I became weak, to win the weak. I have become all things to all men so that by all possible means I might save some." This kind of Incarnational understanding of preaching and ministry is essential for all who utilize new communication forms to convey the old, old message of Scripture.

Jesus was a master at using every means possible to communicate truth. The gospel writers note at least eleven occasions in twenty-two passages in which Jesus directly used physical object lessons to illustrate truth (see Table 2).

Table 2. Jesus' Direct Use of Visual Object Lessons

Occasion	Matthew	Mark	Luke	John
Calling of the fishermen	4:18-22	1:16-20	5:1-11	
Samaritan woman at the well				4:1-26
Jesus is the bread of heaven				6:22-40
Lesson on greatness	18:1-6	9:33-37	9:46-48	
Parable of the rich fool			12:13-21	
Lesson on spiritual blindness				9:35-41
Lesson on seeking honor			14:7-14	
Jesus blesses the children	19:13-15	10:13-16	18:15-17	
Lesson on paying taxes	22:15-22	12:13-17	20:20-26	
Lesson on the widow's offering		12:41-44	21:1-4	
Institution of the Lord's Supper	26:26-29	14:22-25	22:14-23	

This list may initially give only limited evidence for Jesus' use of nonverbal media forms in comparison with the wider scope of his preaching and teaching. However, Table 3 illustrates how the gospels also offer broader evidence of the many times Jesus alludes to metaphors involving people and/or objects that may have been present at the time of his preaching. Taken together with the material in the preceding table, these thirty incidents are cited by the gospel writers in fifty different passages, underscoring the impact of visual methodologies in Jesus' narrative preaching and teaching.

In his classic study titled *The Symbolism of Evil*, Paul Ricoeur offers a phenomenology of symbols that sheds light on the latent power within Jesus' use of the visual imagery of his day. Ricoeur asserts that three dimensions are present in every authentic symbol: the cosmic, the oneiric, and the poetic (10-18). The cosmic dimension underscores that a symbol is something present in the world (e.g., bread and cup); the oneiric dimension points to the dynamic of human imagination and the way a symbol connects to one's psychic histories (e.g., a vivid childhood recollection of the smell of grandmother's freshly baked bread); and, the poetic dimension centers on the way a symbol can be linked artistically to words, songs, and images (e.g., "This is my body"), directing the beholder to become reflective and ultimately to recognize God as the giver of all good things. Gordon Lathrop offers a concise illustration of Ricoeur's phenomenology by examining water as a symbol of religious faith:

> Water is met as the cosmic order, as chaos tamed, as the source of fruitfulness. It is dreamt about as drowning or birth, as washing or sex. And stories are told of the community that lives by the water, defeats the water, survives the water, finds and drinks the water. Such water is received in the biblical poetics and then in Jewish and Christian ritual. But now, for Christians, its full force is broken open [as] a new thing—order and birth and the slaking of thirst where we thought there was only death, in the midst of human life in this world. God comes among us to share our lot and our death, and that sharing is washed over us to make us a new people, witnesses to God's order, alive with God's life. (511)

Likewise, Walter Brueggemann salutes Ricoeur's phenomenology:

> [He] has seen as well as anyone that obedience follows imagination. Our obedience will not venture far beyond or run risks beyond our imagined world. If we wish to have transformed obedience. . . then we must be summoned to an alternative imagination, in order that we may imagine the world and ourselves differently." (*Finally* 85)

Following Ricoeur's model, any of Jesus' uses of metaphor and symbol are key homiletical methods for inspiring human conversion and can be studied at the cosmic, oneiric, and poetic levels. To connect with postmodern culture, preachers are wise to identify not only stories or illustrations that exemplify these levels but also to imaginatively embrace imagery that underscores their reality. Table 3 offers a catalogue of Jesus' use of metaphor in the gospels.

Table 3. Jesus' Use of Metaphor

Occasion	Matthew	Mark	Luke	John
Lesson on salt and light	5:13-16			
Lesson concerning treasures	6:19-24			
Lesson on the narrow gate	7:13-14			
Lesson on a tree and its fruit	7:15-20			
Lesson on a strong foundation	7:21-29			
Jesus our yokefellow	11:28-30			
Parable of the four soils	13:1-9	4:1-9	8:4-8	
Parable of the growing seed		4:26-29		
Parable of the weeds	13:24-30			
Lesson on the light of the body			11:33-36	
Parable of the mustard seed	13:31-32	4:30-34	13:18-19	

Parable of the yeast	13:33-35		13:20-21
Parable of the hidden treasure	13:44		
Parable of the pearl merchant	13:45-46		
Parable of the dragnet	13:47-52		
Lesson on inner defilement	15:1-20	7:1-23	
Lesson on self-denial	16:24-28	8:31-9:1	9:21-27
Parable of the lost sheep	18:12-14		15:1-7
Parable of the lost coin			15:8-10
Lesson on the gate for the sheep			10:7-10

Following the example of Jesus, the Apostle Paul masterfully uses imagery not only in his writing but also in his preaching as well. His example before the Athenians at Mars Hill is an incredible example of imagery turned idolatry and then used instructionally. In this encounter, Paul uses the Greeks' own idols in Acts 17:22-28 to point to the gospel message:

> Paul then stood up in the meeting of the Areopagus and said: "Men of Athens! I see that in every way you are very religious. For as I walked around and looked carefully at your objects of worship, I even found an altar with this inscription: TO AN UNKNOWN GOD. Now what you worship as something unknown I am going to proclaim to you. The God who made the world and everything in it is the Lord of heaven and earth and does not live in temples built by hands. And he is not served by human hands, as if he needed

anything, because he himself gives all men life and breath and everything else. From one man he made every nation of men that they should inhabit the whole earth; and he determined the times set for them and the exact places where they should live. God did this so that men would seek him and perhaps reach out for him and find him, though he is not far from each one of us. 'For in him we live and move and have our being.' As some of your own poets have said, 'We are his offspring.'"

Richard Muow offers the following commentary on Paul's encounter at the Areopagus, observing that the apostle begins by listening, which is the first step in proper exegesis, and then identifies a biblical metaphor to communicate his message:

> I think he presents to us a profoundly biblical and practical missionary methodological model. He did four things, as I see it. First of all, he had studied the Athenian perspective on reality. He knew their writings and was conversant with their poetry. Second, he had discerned an underlining spiritual motif, observing that, "I see that in every way you are very religious." Third, he looked for positive points of contact within their worldview, noting that even their own poets had said, "We are God's offspring." And finally, he invited them to find their fulfillment in the person and work of Jesus Christ. (8)

Paul follows the Aristotelian model, recognizing that the pursuit of understanding moves from what is most familiar to that which is least. Sweet, McLaren, and Haselmayer note that "Symbols are thick texts that mediate our understanding and experience of the world" (151). The Apostle Paul, following Jesus' homiletical form, understands that symbols are the key to believing without seeing. Speaking of Paul, Sidney Greidanus observes that "a metaphor enriches one's understanding. Moreover, metaphors readily lend themselves to elucidation in the sermon so that . . . they begin to function as windows to the truth" (323). By the same token, metaphor can be misused and even abused by preachers. Joel Green and Mark Baker warn biblical interpreters that "Metaphors are two-edged: they reveal and conceal, highlight and hide" (93). Bevan cautions that "The symbol may be an indispensable help so long as you mount beyond it to the thing symbolized; but it is a snare so far as you are caught in it and prevented from rising" (89). Nevertheless, Paul takes comfort in 2 Cor. 4:7b by realizing that even when preachers are at their best, their preaching will always be somewhat limited and imperfect. Preachers today have much to gain from Jesus' and Paul's inclusion of visual elements in their preaching and teaching, especially if they desire to engage visually oriented, postmodern people. Furthermore, the developing thought and work of the Church across two millennia underscores the use of visual media to communicate its message.

Ecclesiastical Precedents

Christians have long affirmed that their preaching, commissioned by the resurrection, is a continuation of Jesus' preaching ministry. As noted in the previous section, this study is rooted in an Incarnational understanding of the preaching event. By this I mean a theological conviction that the immaterial God created the material order, became a human being through the Incarnation of Jesus Christ, and his Holy Spirit remains present in creation and seeks an appeal from every human being through the five human senses. This precept has been embraced by the Church since its earliest days and formed the basis for the final response given to the gnostic heresy and its rejection of the tangible, material world. By affirming the created order and its sensory bridges to humanity, preachers are set free to proclaim God's redeeming work in ways that are first biblical and also meaningful to postmodern people.

Across the centuries, the Church demonstrated incredible creativity in keeping with Jesus' style of communicating through its use of media forms that drew on senses other than the ears only (see Tables 2 and 3). Hugh Kerr's warning to the church from nearly a half century ago still speaks volumes:

> Too much of our . . . Church life is "strictly out of this world" not in a proper eschatological sense but in an unrelated sense. So much of our Sunday worship, our pastoral prayers, our hymns and anthems, our pulpit homilies, our sacramental ceremonies, our vested choirs and divided chancels, our processing and recessing . . . is unrelated to reality... And were it not so soporific and hypnotic, it would not be tolerated by people who are otherwise very much in the world. (295)

Christian history has much to offer twenty-first-century preachers in helping them connect visually with those who are very much a part of the emerging postmodern age. Preachers would be wise to follow the example of the ancient Church, recognizing Jesus' ordination of symbols that linked his followers with their Heavenly Father. In this manner, the early Church retained those symbols that Jesus actually used in his teaching. Likewise, his parables and teaching were collected in the early decades following Jesus' resurrection and ascension and were eventually formalized into the Christian canon. The Church also embraced the common elements of everyday life used by Jesus. Webber notes that "bread, wine, oil and the water of baptism . . . were retained as signs of his continued presence" (*Music* 488).

The use of these symbols by the early Church connects those in contact with them to the powerful human dynamic of imagination, or what Ricoeur calls the oneiric dimension. Alfred North Whitehead, the British mathematician, logician, and philosopher best known for his work in mathematical logic and the philosophy of science, describes symbolism as "no mere idle fancy or corrupt degeneration; it is inherent in the very texture of human life" (61-62). Rob Staples clarifies this connection, contending that imagination itself is a key ingredient of humanity:

> It should be clear that imagination, far from being a flight of fancy, a daydreaming escapism, or the conjuring up of mental images that cannot possibly be true, is the mode of perception that may come closest to defining what it means to be human.. . . If imagination is part of the *imago Dei*, as it surely must be, and not a result of the Fall, is there any reason why it should ever cease? But we can be certain of this: As for us human beings still on earth, who do not yet see "face to face" (1 Cor. 13:12), reality is mediated through myriads of oblique angles and colors and shapes and textures in the fabric of creation. (59-60)

Likewise, Walter Brueggemann observes that this transforming dynamic is still at work two thousand years after the birth of the Church:

> [P]eople in fact change by the offer of new models, images, and pictures of how the pieces of life fit together—models, images, and pictures that characteristically have the particularity of narrative to carry them. Transformation is the slow, steady process of inviting each other into a counterstory about God, world, neighbor, and self. This slow, steady process has as counterpoint the subversive process of unlearning and disengaging from a story we no longer find to be credible or adequate. (*Texts* 24-25)

Like Jesus and Paul, the early Church connected the human imagination to God in its worship and preaching using a variety of multisensory means. The liturgical use of incense in worship appeals to both vision and smell. Likewise, baptism engages worshipers through tactile, aural, and visual means. Perhaps the most dramatic example of the use of media forms other than the spoken word is the sacrament of the Lord's Supper, which engages through all five senses those who partake it in one sitting.

The early father Tertullian takes an iconoclastic view of images, and his position marks the early Christian centuries. Clement and Origen build on Tertullian's foundation by incorporating classical Greek philosophies in their development of Christian theology while rejecting the visual aesthetic of Greek culture. Clement claims the second commandment prohibits "the making of any carved or molten or moulded or painted image and representation, in order that we might not direct our attention to sensible objects, but might proceed to the intelligential" (qtd. in Goethals 14). Goethals cites the reason behind the Alexandrian Father's aversion for the visual:

> Clement, echoing the Platonic view, also maintains that images are not "true." Human beings are images of God—but an image of the image, the statues made in the likeness of human beings and far removed from the truth, appear only as a "fleeting impression." He considered preoccupation with images as "madness in a life." (14)

Origen holds that imagery is likened to pagan worship, dragging down the soul rather than directing the worshiper to God's invisible reality (Bevan 107-108). Saint Augustine presumes that religious art is primarily decorative and lacking theological content. William Diebold records Augustine's attempt at subordinating images to words:

> For a picture is looked at in a different way from that in which a writing is looked at. When thou hast seen a picture, to have seen it is the whole thing; when thou seest a writing, this is not the whole, since thou art reminded also to read it. (106)

Despite these views, not to mention the fact that most of the symbolic art created in the first three centuries of the Church has not survived, several clues still point out that the earliest generations of Christians used symbols in their worship and teaching. Bread, fish, and the *Chi-Rho* monogram appear frequently in ancient places of worship. The Roman catacombs of the late second and third centuries, as well as a baptistery in a Syrian house church called Dura-Europas provide important, yet admittedly elementary examples of pre-Constantinian evidence of an iconic aesthetic in the early Church. Although these graphic representations are simplistic, they are, nevertheless, figural representations of the Christian faith located in the context of their liturgical life. Webber describes the wall paintings found at Dura-Europas:

> Next to Adam and Eve hiding their nakedness we see Christ carrying the lost sheep on his shoulders. Further on, the holy women are making their way to the tomb carrying torches... Then some miracles are depicted: the paralytic, healed by Christ, carrying away his bed; and Jesus walking on the water in the storm, stretching out his hand to St. Peter. We also find the woman of Samaria at the well, and David, who has just slain Goliath. (*Music* 488-89)

When Christianity became the official state religion as a result of Constantine's conversion in the fourth century, most of the populace was unable to read. Faced with the pressing need to communicate to an empire of Christians who had been converted by statute, the Church was forced to accommodate its teaching methods for those who were accustomed to visual representations as their basis for comprehension. Over the centuries that followed, Christian art and ecclesiastical architecture became vehicles for the indoctrination of preliterate catechumenates through the use of religious sculpture, stained glass, artwork, icons, friezes, doors, and furnishings.

With the reign of the Holy Roman Empire, the visual arts took their ascendancy in the Church. Rich mosaics and elaborate paintings became more than visual narratives only; instead, they were designed to reinforce the teachings of the faith by complementing the liturgy. For over a millennium, the Church based its use of Christian imagery on three issues. Chief among them was the instruction of the illiterate peasant masses, who Saint Felix describes as "not devoid of religion but not able to read" (qtd. in Goethals 15). A second use of Christian imagery was to activate the message of Scripture in the memory and imagination. As the Dominican Fra Michele da Carcano observes, "Images were introduced because many people cannot retain in their memories what they hear, but they do remember if they see images" (qtd. in Baxandall 41). Finally, images arouse devotion through the vividness of what is seen rather than through what is heard only. Writing to artists, Michael Baxandall relates that the painter was considered a professional visualizer of holy stories in partnership with the preacher. Each took notice of the other, for as Baxandall observes, "The preacher and painter were *repetiteur* to each other" (49). He goes on to describe the partnership between preachers and artists:

> If you commute these three reasons for images into instructions for the beholder, it amounts to using pictures as respectively lucid, vivid and readily accessible stimuli to meditation on the Bible and the lives of Saints. If you convert them into a brief for the painter, they carry an expectation that the picture should tell its story in a clear way for

the simple and in an eye-catching and memorable way for the forgetful, and with full use of all the emotional resources of the sense of sight, the most powerful as well as the most precise of the senses. (43)

By the end of the sixth century, aniconic attitudes rose within the Church. As a result, Gregory the Great sanctioned the use of imagery while cautioning against venerating Christian art–an attitude that continues to shape Western Christendom. When Serena's, the bishop of Marseilles, became an iconoclast and destroyed the imagery in his church, Gregory cautioned him as follows:

> It is one thing to offer homage to (*adorare*) a picture and quite another thing to learn, by way of a story told in a picture, to what homage ought to be offered... If anyone desires to make images, do not forbid him; only prohibit by all the means in your power the worshipping of images. (qtd. in Goethals 23)

Gregory insists that "icons are for the unlettered what the Sacred Scriptures are for the lettered" (qtd. in Clendenin 33).

Literally translated as "books of the poor," the proliferation of the *Biblia Pauperum* could accurately be called the "Poor Man's Bible" of the fifteenth-century European Church. Produced inexpensively from impressions on wooden blocks carved in relief, these forty-leaf blockbooks originated in the Netherlands where the art of woodcarving flourished. Serving as a transitory media form between hand-lettered manuscripts and books printed by movable type, each page of the *Biblia Pauperum* instructed the illiterate chiefly through biblical iconography. Arranged typologically with Old Testament characters and events foreshadowing their more prominent New Testament counterparts, the *Biblia Pauperum* assumes the unity of both testaments. It chronicles the major themes of both the Old and New Testaments, offering a systematic overview of the message of Scripture in visual terms. They attempt to communicate the development of God's eternal purposes through imagery and metaphor rather than by words primarily. Each page is designed both vertically and horizontally in cruciform as shown in Figures 1 and 2.

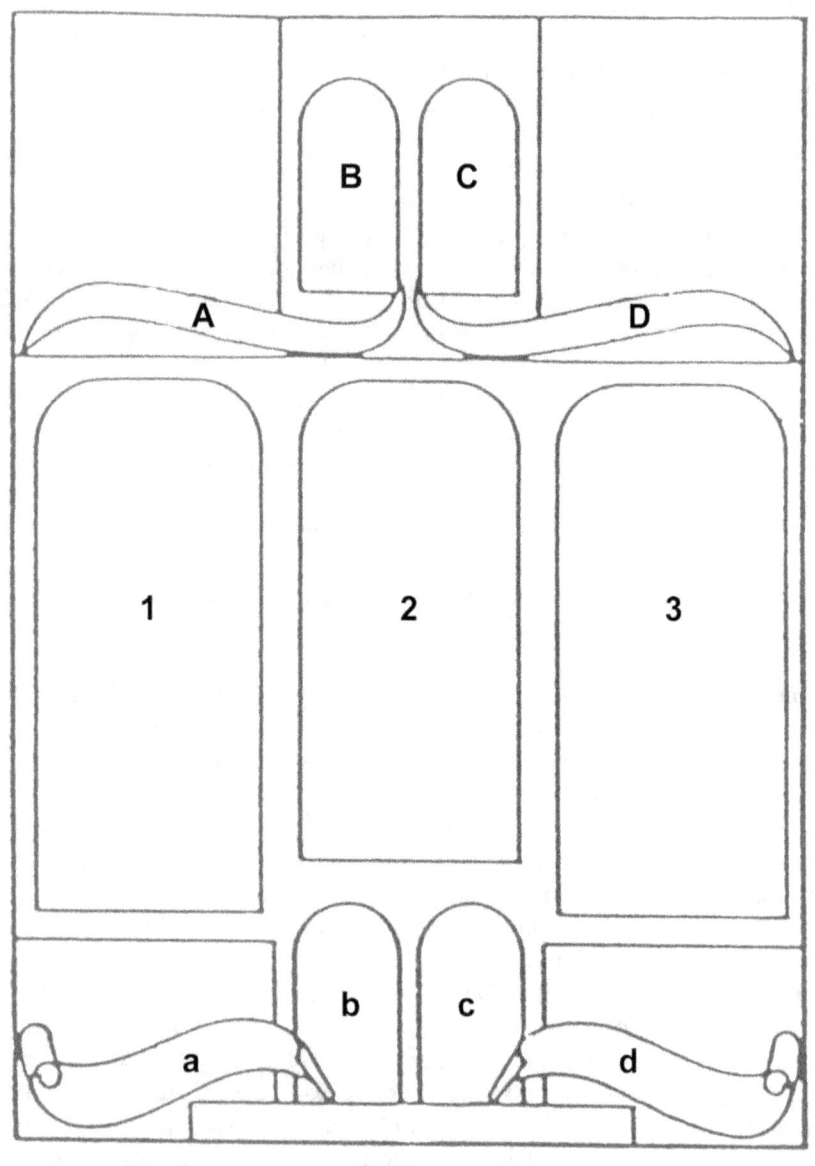

Source: Latriola and Smeltz 13

Figure 1. *Biblia Pauperum Blockbook* Template

Figure 1 illustrates how the primary focus of each leaf is a centralized triptych featuring a dominant New Testament theme (**2**) and bordered on each side by supporting scenes predominantly from the Old Testament (**1** and **3**). Each leaf within the *Biblia Pauperum* is designed to resemble the gallery of arches above the side-aisle vaulting in a Gothic cathedral. Featured above the triptych in the top third of each page are two prophets or patriarchs (**B** and **C**), each framed by a pillar and holding scrolls (**A** and **D**) that cite verses from both testaments. These are related typologically to the prominent story in the middle panel (**2**) of the triptych. Old Testament paraphrases and interpretive commentary fill the empty spaces at the top and bottom of each page. The bottom portion of each page includes the inscribed names (**a** and **d**) of two additional Old Testament figures (**b** and **c**) whose stories point to the dominant New Testament theme featured on that leaf. Albert Latriola and John Smeltz describe the placement of characters within each plate:

> The personages, who become virtual witnesses of the fulfillment of their prophecies or of the episodes in which they participated, thus escape the temporal limitations of their own lives, develop a Christ-centered view of history, and acquire insight into the enigmas of the Old Testament. (7)

The authors go on to say that each page of the blockbook also strived to inspire the spiritual passions of those who looked at them:

> In addition to its selective exposition of Scripture by typology and iconography, the *Biblia Pauperum* also aimed to edify its audience concerning the life of Christ. Coupled with intellectual understanding, in other words, was an emotional response of devotion and gratitude for Christ's ministry of Redemption, emphasized in scenes of the Passion and Crucifixion. This dual purpose of exposition and edification, effectively commingled and efficiently executed in the blockbook, was aptly suited to the "poor man"–both to the level of understanding and to the threshold of emotional response of the common folk. (Latriola 9-10)

Figure 2 is one of the most prominent leafs in the *Biblia Pauperum*, illustrating the crucifixion of Christ. At the foot of the cross, Jesus' mother Mary faints into the arms of the Apostle John while a Roman Centurion points heavenward, acknowledging that Jesus surely was the Messiah (Matt. 27:54). The left panel of the triptych illustrates that the crucifixion is the divine fulfillment of Abraham's test in Genesis 22 regarding his willingness to offer his own son Isaac as a sacrificial lamb to God. The right panel grows out of

Israel's wilderness wanderings in Numbers 21:6-9. This passage features the plight of the Israelites who had been bitten by serpents in the wilderness. In the story, Moses instructs every snakebite victim to look with faith upon a bronze serpent raised on a pole for their deliverance. Jesus himself cites this passage in John 3:14-15 to foretell his own eventual death and the redeeming power he offers both rich and poor, literate and illiterate.

Source: *Latriola and Smeltz 39*

Figure 2. Christ Is Crucified

The value of typological interpretations of the Old Testament is that they recognize the historical continuity of revelation and God's redemptive work in history. Likewise, they take seriously Jesus' own declaration in John 5:39 that the Hebrew Scriptures bear witness to him. By the same token, typology can be problematic when it devalues the Old Testament as something less than God's revelation to Israel, limiting the Hebrew Scriptures to nothing more than a book of signs and incomplete symbols. An interpreter's failure to recognize the contexts and historicity of the Old Testament accounts can undercut a proper understanding of the role of the Hebrew Scriptures in preparing God's people for the Messiah's advent, when the Word became flesh in the fullness of time. The same challenge remains for preachers who utilize visual media in their preaching. Media, as well as the sermon itself, must find its foundation in Scripture. Failure to do so risks elevating media above the biblical metaphors alive in the text.

Returning to historical developments, the twelfth century brought the iconic controversy into sharp contrast. Suger, the Abbot of Saint Dennis, advocated the use of visual arts in celebrating the gospel. By the same token, Bernard of Clairvaux, who was himself a contemporary of Suger's, reformed the Cistercian order through aesthetic simplicity. Goethals observes that "[b]oth Suger and Bernard were symbolists, yet their activities and attitudes resulted in contradictory kinds of Christian aesthetics" (24). Suger advocated the philosophy of *via affirmativa*, which holds that sacred material representations can inspire devotion. Bernard's dedication to the Rule of Saint Benedict resulted in a focus on Christian simplicity that rejected not only the use of imagery but also the majestic architectural form and scale advocated by Suger. In spite of their simple, functional forms, Bernard's utilitarian monasteries nevertheless speak vividly: "Light upon simple surfaces, patterns of repeated geometric shapes, the compelling vertical and horizontal rhythms of support and buttresses–all, despite the lack of images, create an aesthetic vocabulary" (qtd. in Goethals 37). In the end, Bernard's *via negativa* had limited impact outside the Cistercian order and the use of imagery became more widespread in the middle Ages.

Beginning in the twelfth century and extending well into the sixteenth century, Gothic cathedrals were constructed in Medieval Europe as eloquent symbols of the majesty and power of the Christian faith. Wealthy landowners were called upon for large sums of capital, the middle classes provided skilled labor, and the peasant class performed the unskilled labor needed to construct these massive churches. The grand scope of construction often surpassed the life spans of the artisans themselves.

By the thirteenth century, Gregory's influence continued to cast a long shadow on Christian thought regarding religious imagery. Drawing from Gregory, Thomas Aquinas reflected that worshipers are not drawn to the images themselves but to the reality they represent. Thus Christ, rather than the image, is venerated. Late medieval preachers were also skilled in the art of movement, often drawing from a repertoire of gestures known to worshipers from popular forms of Christian art. Margaret Miles indicates that "[m]anuals of such gestures existed, providing a stylized body language that accompanied and heightened the verbal communication" (68).

By the time of the Enlightenment, the Western Church was well on its way to embracing more rational rather than sensory expressions in worship and preaching. Clendenin states that "[w]hile the East wanted to *see* [original emphasis] the Word in images, the West insisted on *hearing* [original emphasis] it in the spoken word. Begun by a cadre of intellectuals, the Reformation placed tremendous weight on the written word" (33). Myron Gilmore clarifies the cultural transformation from visual to textual literacy and its magnitude on the advent of the Reformation:

> The invention and development of printing with moveable types brought about the most radical transformation in the conditions of intellectual life in the history of Western Civilization... Its effects were sooner or later felt in every department of human activity. (186)

Arthur Dickens expands on the importance of Gutenburg's press to the Protestant Reformation:

> In relation to the spread of religious ideas it seems difficult to exaggerate the significance of the Press, without which a revolution of this magnitude could scarcely have been consummated. Unlike the Wycliffe and Waldensian controversies, Lutheranism was from the first the child of the printed book, and through this vehicle Luther was able to make exact, standardized and ineradicable impressions on the mind of Europe. (51)

The aniconic reforms that accompanied the sixteenth-century Protestant Reformation well exceeded Bernard's objections. Andreas Carlstadt disparaged religious art and music, while Martin Luther stood apart from his contemporaries by retaining the value of these media forms for religious instruction. Genevan John Calvin and Ulrich Zwingli of Zurich emphasized Scripture as the Christian's sole guide to faith. They taught that anything placed between the faithful pilgrim and God–including not only imagery, but material possessions, power, and prestige–encouraged idolatry. Their emphasis on the reading and preaching of Scripture became a hallmark of Protestant religion. Churches under their charge were stripped of their images and whitewashed.

Ironically, the Protestant iconoclasts also utilized visual means to communicate their theology—in this case through their absence of imagery. For example, the eighteenth-century meetinghouses of New England reflect their theological forefathers through designs incorporating austere interiors, plain white clapboard exteriors, and clear, rather than ornate stained-glass, windows. While sterile, all of these are visual markers nonetheless. Furthermore, Calvinism's aniconic rationality impacted the visual arts beyond the reach of the Church as Goethals observes:

> Rembrandt frequently used religious subjects in his paintings and etchings, but there was no place for them in the churches of seventeenth-century Holland. His Flemish contemporary Peter Paul Rubens, on the other hand, moved in royal circles and was sought out for his elaborate decoration of Baroque churches in Roman Catholic countries throughout Europe. (51)

With no demand for their masterpieces in Dutch churches, artists grew dependent upon secular patrons resulting in more artistic innovations of landscape and portraiture rather than those centering on Christian themes.

In the past century or so, a wide variety of new media forms have been introduced to the Church. Jeanne Halgren Kilde notes that proscenium arches and gallery boxes found their way into ecclesiastical architecture in the late nineteenth century:

> [C]hurches installed individual upholstered, flip-up opera seats in place of pews. First M. E. in Baltimore featured rows of such seats with hat racks placed handily under each. In addition, as the popularity of lantern slide shows grew in the 1890s, designers installed projection booths in the backs of their sanctuaries. Clarence H. Blackhall's rebuilding of the Tremont Temple in Boston in 1894-1896, for instance, was among the first instances of a permanent projection booth being inserted into a sanctuary. As the twentieth century progressed, accommodations for visual technologies increased. (129-30)

While some churches took a more progressive view of such technologies, they were not without controversy, however. For example, the Church of the

Nazarene, the denomination that planted New Hope and of which I am a member and ordained elder, has struggled historically with the place of many of these new media forms both in ministry and in the private lives of its membership. One cannot consider the use of visual media in a Nazarene congregation today without considering the historic position of the denomination against their very use.

Stan Ingersol serves as denominational archivist for the Church of the Nazarene in Kansas City, Missouri, a position he has held since 1985. In an interview, Ingersol talked at length about the denomination's historic position on the medium of cinema. From its founding in 1908, the Church of the Nazarene banned its members from attending the movie theater. In an early edition of the *Manual*, the denominational discipline for the Church of the Nazarene, members were first admonished to avoid every kind of evil, including: "[s]uch songs, literature, and entertainments as are not to the glory of God; the avoidance of the theater, the ball room, the circus and like places; also lotteries and games of chance; looseness and impropriety of conduct" (Walker, Hosley, and Girvin 69). Interestingly, these prohibitions were listed even before a series of more positive general principles for Christian living. After outlining the importance of avoiding these specified forms of evil, the first Nazarenes were secondarily encouraged to do "that which is enjoined in the Word of God, which is both our rule of faith and practice" (69).

Randall Davey, who served on the denominational committee overseeing matters of social action in 1989, provides an historical review of popular Nazarene opinions on the cinema. His article reviews materials published in the *Herald of Holiness*, the official publication of the Church of the Nazarene. Davey reveals that even in its earliest days, the denomination struggled to various degrees over the movie issue:

> Some Nazarenes asked, "Is it wrong?" while others attended. One response, titled "An Overgrown Evil," appeared in the August 7, 1912 edition. The editor urged censorship of the fast-growing industry, something New York City had already done. He concurred with a growing consensus that the movies had a demoralizing tendency on viewers. Psychologists of that day, he reported, were already assuming a cause and effect relationship between the content of movies and behavior patterns of the viewers…
>
> In July of 1914, Rev. C. E. Cornell offered a counterposition in an article published in the *Herald* titled "The Devil's Harvest." While agreeing that the moving-picture theater is the most subtle form of

> temptation ever invented, Cornell argued that it was indeed possible to use the invention for Christ's sake. He simply raised the question whether this "marvelous invention" would be monopolized by the devil to damn millions, or whether the church should use it to elevate, instruct, and save the masses.
>
> By May 3, 1916, a terse editorial appeared, saying that "a desire for those forms of pleasure and entertainment which are distinctively worldly, and which have immoral associations and tendencies, proves a lack of knowledge of salvation as it is in Jesus." (27-28)

Despite the debate, the denomination's official position on movies remained untouched for nearly seventy years.

In 1976, Nazarenes reconfigured the *Manual* for organizational purposes, moving the ban on movies to a new section called the "Special Rules." Here the General Assembly sought to offer a fuller explanation of its stand against worldly entertainments such as the film industry:

> We hold specifically that the following practices should be avoided: entertainments that are subversive of Christian morals. Our people should govern themselves by three principles. One is the Christian stewardship of leisure time. A second principle is the recognition of the Christian obligation to apply the highest moral standards to the home. Since we are living in a day of great moral confusion in which we face the potential encroachment of the evils of the day into the sacred precincts of our homes through various avenues such as current literature, radio, and television, it is essential that the most rigid safeguards be observed. The third principle is the obligation to witness against social evils by appropriate forms of influence, and the refusal to patronize and thereby lend influence to the industries which are known to be purveyors of this kind of entertainment. This would include the avoidance of the motion picture theater (cinema), together with such other commercial ventures which feature the cheap, the violent, or the sensual and pornographic and thus undermine God's standard of holiness of heart and life. (*Manual/1976* 44-45)

Four years later, the general assembly retained the above statement and added a biblical basis for their position, claiming Romans 14:7-13, 1 Corinthians 10:31-33, Ephesians 5:1-18, Philippians 4:8-9, and 1 Peter 1:13-17 for support.

With the proliferation of new media forms in the 1980s like videocassettes and cable television, the Nazarene Special Rules struggled to keep pace with technology. In 1989, the general assembly was held in Indianapolis, by far the most conservative region of the United States for Nazarenes. Prior to the general assembly, the denomination's social action committee was asked to study the issue regarding movies. According to Ingersol, the committee's recommendation would have eliminated any ban because it had become a lost cause in their mind. The Special Rule on movies was "morality based on geography" because it banned the movie theater specifically yet was silent about viewing movies at home. According to the social action committee, the denomination needed an entertainment ethic rather than a ban. When the matter came before the special resolutions committee, which was usually a formality, it ran into fierce opposition by the hometown crowd.

By the time the resolution came to the general assembly floor, the superintendent of the Indianapolis district vehemently opposed the social action committee's recommendation. Instead, he amended the legislation by trying to distinguish between Christian film producers and those in Hollywood. In the end, Ingersol indicated that the verbal amendment, which was approved by the general assembly, was nevertheless grammatically incorrect. The General Assembly's editing committee determined that a literal reading of the amendment could be understood to say that Nazarenes were opposed to pornographic films unless they were produced by Christian producers.

From that point, Ingersol noted that the denominational position on movies could be compared with Judges 17:6 when Israel had no king and "everyone did what was right in their own eyes." Popular practice shaped denominational interpretation. By common consent, Nazarenes have done away with their ban on movies.

Today the Special Rules are gone. The current *Manual* statement can be found in a section now retitled "The Covenant of Christian Conduct." It includes the following clarification, now expanding media even further to include virtual technologies. The current statement also encourages younger Nazarenes to take an Incarnational position in the world by positively impacting the very industry with whom the church battled for so many decades:

> Because we are living in a day of great moral confusion in which we face the potential encroachment of the evils of the day into the sacred precincts of our homes through various avenues such as

current literature, radio, television, personal computers, and the Internet, it is essential that the most rigid safeguards be observed to keep our homes from becoming secularized and worldly. However, we hold that entertainment that endorses and encourages holy living and affirms scriptural values should be affirmed and encouraged. We especially encourage our young people to use their gifts in media and the arts to influence positively this pervasive part of culture. (*Manual/2001-2005* 45-46)

Literary Precedents

One of the challenges facing twenty-first-century preaching is the need to bring the message of the "Good Book" to life in a congregational culture that draws less information from linear sources like the printed page in favor of other more interactive, visual, nonlinear communication forms. In an interview with Leadership Network, Calvin Miller underscores the preacher's need to understand this new literacy of culture:

> It's more about how people listen than how preachers preach... This is a day and age when you really need to think about and study to whom you are speaking... I try to understand the importance of metaphor, language, and story. (Leadership Network 1)

Preaching with contemporary forms is not enough, however. To be true to their call, twenty-first-century preachers must ground their communication in Scriptures that were written to other cultures, are roughly two thousand or more years old, and were initially related through an oral rather than written tradition. With this in mind, preachers must recognize their role as translators of the biblical message into their contemporary context. Richard Rohrbaugh observes that this kind of cross-cultural reading of the Bible is not a matter of choice:

> Since the Bible is a Mediterranean document written for Mediterranean readers, it presumes the cultural resources and worldview available to a reader socialized in the Mediterranean world. This means that for all non-Mediterraneans, including all Americans, reading the Bible is always an exercise in cross-cultural communication. It is only a question of doing it poorly or doing it well. (1)

To further complicate matters, preachers must not only do battle with the distance existing between the initial oral tradition and its written form found in Scripture; they must also recognize how the media revolutions experienced over the first two millennia from story to manuscript to text to video impinge upon each other. Thomas Boomershine states the case plainly: "Media changes constitute a revolution in consciousness" (*Peter's Denial* 49), and Miller asserts that "the church that reaches the unevangelicized world will speak the street language of encounter" (*Marketplace* 39). Preachers must consider how to convey the biblical message, which was originally told to a predominately preliterate people, in ways that will engage a growing audience of essentially postliterate people who prefer not to gather most of their information by reading.

Forms of Literacy

Lucretia Yaghjian observes that an important dialogue is taking place in this arena through a study of ancient and contemporary understandings of reading theory and literacy forms. Her point is that people tend to assume the primacy of the written text as it is found in the Bible today rather than understanding that the cultures of the Old and New Testaments were thoroughly committed to the spoken word–even after the biblical material was preserved in manuscript form:

> If we are to "understand" reading in the cultural world of the NT, we must first take off the conceptual lenses through which we habitually read, and begin to read with our ears as well as our eyes. Second, we must change our societal image of reading from a private rendezvous with the printed page to a public broadcast of oral and/or written communication. Finally, we must revise our culturally conditioned biased definitions of "literacy" and "illiteracy," and allow the biblical documents to spell out their own contextual ones. (207)

Yaghjian distinguishes between four forms of cultural literacy, basing each one on biblical precedent, in order to clarify the interaction between oral and literate processes in Mediterranean antiquity. These literacy forms lay the groundwork for an understanding of postliteracy that follows.

Auraliteracy. Yaghjian begins by noting that this form of literacy is the least technical and most inclusive of all literacy strategies, involving the practice of hearing something read as when Paul writes for oral delivery in 2 Corinthians 1:13: "For we write you nothing other than what you can read and also understand." In this passage, as well as in Ephesians 3:4 and Colossians 4:16, Paul's intended audience is an auraliterate mixture of both readers and hearers. Auraliterate reading is the practice of reading texts that are meant to be communicated aurally—that is, to the ear. Jensen recalls an encounter with auraliteracy as a Lutheran missionary:

> Until very recently the priests in the Orthodox Church received a rather simple training. What they learned most of all was how to recite the liturgy perfectly. The illiterate worshiper expected a certain sound and that sound could not be changed. (20)

Jensen's example is very similar to what my very young daughters experienced when they wanted to "read" a Dr. Seuss book with me. They knew from experience what a Cat in the Hat book should sound like even without being able to read a single sentence. Their auraliteracy enabled them even to go so far as to know if their father inadvertently skipped a page, simply because the story did not "sound" right as they "read" along in the familiar text.

Oraliteracy. Oraliteracy is reading that is orally performed but that is given some textual context. Properly understood, oraliteracy is a subset of literacy. Yaghjian notes that oraliterate readers recite memorized text, even though they may not be able to recognize every letter. They, like the Apostle Paul's young apprentice Timothy, know the sacred writings by heart (2 Tim. 3:14-15) and can recite them "with the natural proficiency of people brought up in an oral environment" (208). Following the previous analogy drawn from my own family life, oraliteracy could be seen in my oldest daughter as her reading confidence grew. While her vocabulary had admittedly expanded, she also knew the context for many of her stories so well that her reading at times included phrases of her own making. These words were not literally on the page; nevertheless, they fit the context of the story.

Oculiteracy. This form of literacy involves both the eyes and ears in the reading process. It involves decoding letters by the eye and comprehension of the latent ideas through the hearing of what is read. Oculiterate readers do not understand what is written when they first see the words but comprehend it after the reading is finally heard. Only by hearing decoded writing does the reader understand. This form of literacy is prevalent in early readers who cannot yet grasp at first glance that c-a-t means cat, but as they hear the phonetic sounds put together, they register the appropriate meaning. By the same token, Paul Achtemeier makes a strong case that this type of literacy was the predominant form in the Greco-Roman world for centuries, noting that "the oral environment was so pervasive that *no* [original emphasis] writing occurred that was not vocalized" (15). He expands his point at greater length:

> Most interesting from our perspective, and perhaps least generally understood, is the fact that even solitary readers, reading only to themselves, read aloud.... Reading was oral performance whenever it occurred and in whatever circumstances. Late antiquity knew nothing of the "silent, solitary reader." (16-17)

Oculiterate reading is the process of hearing spoken words that are read from a manuscript. In the New Testament, this form of literacy is demonstrated by Jesus' public reading from the scroll in the synagogue at Nazareth in Luke 4:16-20.

Scribaliteracy. Scribaliteracy is best seen in Acts 8:32-35 when Philip interprets Isaiah 53 to the Ethiopian eunuch. Yaghjian adds that scribaliteracy is technical reading for professional or religious purposes, generally on behalf of a particular interpretive community. Not surprisingly, she indicates that it belonged to the privileged few who were involved in the interpretive activity of the religious and civil scribes:

> Scribaliterate reading embraces oculiterate, oraliterate, and auraliterate reading in its repertoire, and is exemplified par excellence by Luke (and other NT authors), whose scribal hand claims authoritative status for his reading of the tradition [in Luke 1:4]. (209)

Some will argue that Yaghjian is splitting hairs and that auraliteracy and oraliteracy are simply variations of a classic definition of illiteracy as one who can neither read nor write with understanding. Likewise, others may misconstrue Yaghjian's understanding of oculiteracy and scribaliteracy simply as gradations on the continuum of literacy. Instead, Yaghjian's point is that people cannot understand ancient biblical texts today without recognizing the influence these various forms of literacy had on those who initially conveyed the oral traditions, those who wrote them down in manuscript form, and those who heard or read them in the first century of the Church. Furthermore, the influence of postmodern cultural developments, particularly as they relate to the way Americans increasingly gather information by means other than the printed page, have the potential of affecting how they understand the Bible in the future.

Postliteracy. Regardless of whether the date in history is set in the present age or two millennia ago, this section within the literature review demonstrates that literacy takes shape in specific cultural and social settings. Functional illiteracy remains a problem to some extent even today in a literature-saturated culture like the United States. The National Institute for Literacy reports that slightly more than one-fifth of American adults today read at or below the level needed to earn a living wage (par. 1). By the same token, Barna observes that "[d]espite the fears that America will become a nation that does not read, two-thirds of all adults interviewed in January 1992 said they had read part of a book, other than the Bible, during the prior week (*Barna Report* 124). On the one hand, a portion of Americans are functionally illiterate; on the other, the publishing and bookselling industries continue to flourish today. Considering the explosive growth of retail booksellers like Barnes and Noble, Borders, and the online megamerchant Amazon.com, many critics have difficulty appreciating that Americans are becoming increasingly postliterate. Many believe that if postliteracy is a reality, the prevalence of books and booksellers should be on the decline. Yet Jason Epstein, former editorial director of Random House and cofounder of *The New York Review of Books*, disagrees:

> These new technologies will not, in my opinion, preclude retail bookstores. Shops like the Tattered Cover and Northshire or the surviving chain store branches will flourish for the same reasons that cinemas flourish despite television and videotapes. New technologies do not erase the past, but build upon it. (168-69)

The issue is not so much that most people today cannot read or that they have given up on reading; instead, postliteracy focuses on the claim that the culture today gains less of its information from the printed page than it did in ages past. Without question, large audiences of people will continue to prefer the literate environment of their upbringing. Twenty-first-century preachers are called upon to share the whole gospel with the whole world, regardless if they are illiterate, literate, or postliterate.

Babin and Iannone offer a fascinating approach to the preacher's challenge in something he calls "stereo catechesis":

> I believe that, in catechesis, the time has finally come for us to function with both hemispheres of the brain. Until the 16th century, catechesis functioned essentially in "mono 1," with the right-brain hemisphere predominating. Since Gutenberg and the Council of Trent, it has functioned essentially in "mono 2," with the left-brain hemisphere dominating. But these times have passed and, although there are still preponderances, we ought now to function definitively

in stereo, both in order to enter into the truth of Christ and to respect human wholeness. (6)

The implications of this catechetical shift are making themselves apparent in the Church, especially with regard to biblical preaching and its traditional focus on left-brain hemisphere dominance with its emphasis on written words.

In a provocative book titled *Why Nobody Learns Much of Anything at Church*, Thom and Joani Schultz share their discoveries from a poll of adult church attenders:

- . . . 12 percent say they usually remember the message.

- 87 percent say their mind wanders during sermons.

- 35 percent say the sermons they hear are too long.

- 11 percent of women and 5 percent of men credit sermons as their primary source of knowledge about God. (189)

The Schultzes go on to cite a University of California study indicating that words themselves only carry a minimal part (roughly 7 percent) of the message. Instead, the speaker's vocal variety, energy, and inflections carry 38 percent of the message. The remaining 55 percent of the message is carried by the speaker's appearance, gestures, movement, and visual aids (191). Christian communicators need an understanding of postliteracy and the role visual media play effective modes for conveying biblical truth to an increasingly postliterate culture.

Homiletical Precedents

The age of Enlightenment and its marriage to the Reformation gave birth to a corresponding passion for rational thought. David Buttrick observes that over the past three centuries since the first Protestant pilgrims made their way to North America, the cultural scaffolding supporting American Christianity has shifted from an understanding of the nation as God's new Israel to a moralistic understanding of civil religion to an ever more modern view of the individual under God (422). Over time, many today claim that twentieth-century Protestant structures that were built upon the Enlightenment are now caving in like a top-heavy Tower of Babel. Today's postmodern, postscientific, postliterate mind-set is sifting through the wreckage left in the wake of a collapsing rationalistic world. Preachers now face the challenge of communicating the gospel to a world in process, caught between the now and the not yet.

In response to the Church's new mission field, Buttrick calls for an auditing of the Church, urging the so-called "people of one book" to admit they have actually kept two sets of ledgers: one in the form of the Bible and the other written in the rational language of the Enlightenment. As the cultural pendulum swings to a postmodern, postscientific, postliterate understanding of life, this project urges the Church to re-embrace Jesus' multisensory approach to preaching by incorporating other forms of media into the sermon in order to engage people with the transforming power of the gospel. While the subject matter and purpose of sermons vary in many respects from other forms of communication, preachers have much to gain from an understanding of contemporary communication theory. The Church must once again embrace the inclusion of visual media in its proclamation of the gospel in order to reach postmodern, postliterate people.

Postmodern people assert that they are different from their modern predecessors. Accustomed to fuller experiences encompassing the breadth of all five senses and having been raised in front of the television, many experts claim they are keenly attuned to the visual rather than the left-brained methods that continue to dominate contemporary preaching. They have little patience, not to mention appreciation, for the rational, linear presentation model that pervades most pulpits today. Tim Celek and Dieter Zander state their case against linear preaching plainly:

> In terms of making Jesus relevant to this generation, forty-five minutes of staring at a talking head in a church service is not going to cut it... What they're looking for is not something to entertain them, but something to engage them. (67)

At New Hope Church, I attempt to engage our congregation by harnessing the power of metaphors within Scripture and translating them as visual counterparts to the Bible's written text and my own spoken words. Len Wilson, who originally inspired me to adopt a visual homiletic, points out that "[t]he purpose of a metaphor in worship is to provide a multifaceted point of entry by representing the basic ideas of the biblical story in a language that the culture can understand" (Wilson and Moore 36).

Rather than scanning a Bible text for potential alliterative devices as many highly literate preachers do, or diving into an in-depth study of the elements of form and style used by the writer, my own hermeneutical research begins elsewhere. Lexicons, concordances, grammars, word-study books, Bible dictionaries, commentaries, and a whole host of other interpretive tools all have their place in the process; however, my own analysis begins, not with the above-mentioned tools, but with a quest in the Scripture itself for the central idea of the passage under review. Once this exegetical idea is captured, my interpretive method moves to the identification of the dominant biblical metaphor within the passage. From this foundation, which is rooted in Scripture and framed in a biblical metaphor, I use other interpretive tools while attempting to follow the admonition popularly attributed to Saint Francis of Assisi: "Preach the gospel at all times. If necessary, use words." While Francis is most likely referring primarily to social action, the visual interpretation offered above has served me well in my own attempt to move away from propositional sermons toward preaching that is more experiential and relational while still remaining unwaveringly biblical.

Some preachers wince at the thought of locating visual markers within the written words of Scripture. Wilson and Moore share their own experiences in this regard:

> Somebody said to me once at a conference, "Why don't you focus less on metaphors and more on the Word of God?" The question gave me a wonderful opportunity to talk about how often the word of God is itself metaphor. The burning bush is God in a metaphor. The dove is the Holy Spirit in a metaphor. The mustard seed is a metaphor for faith. In fact the Word is more often communicated in metaphors than any other way that I can recall! We innately grasp understanding when a concept or object is compared (and simultaneously contrasted) to some other idea or thing in our experience. This process is the basis for abstract thinking. (36)

Leveraging a metaphor within the biblical story involves much more than explaining an idea in Scripture, however. Jensen differentiates between metaphors of illustration and metaphors of participation:

> I am convinced that metaphors of illustration do not serve the living gospel of our Lord Jesus Christ as well as metaphors of participation. We ought to tell stories through which the realities of the text become the realities of the hearer. (113)

To illustrate, I offer an example of how visual media can partner with the spoken word, based on an example from my own preaching. During my first meeting with my research and reflection team, I asked those present to recall as many of my sermons as they could, putting stars alongside their favorites. The most popular sermon mentioned was popularly termed the "Michelangelo sermon."

This sermon was one of four messages I preached in February 2002 as part of a series titled "MasterWorks." Each week, I used a masterpiece from daVinci, Michelangelo, or Rembrandt to connect the congregation with the message of Scripture. The final week, I featured the work of an unknown individual named Max Klein. Klein is best known for creating the CraftMaster paint-by-numbers kit. In this sermon, I called the congregation to open the canvas of their lives to God and allow him to fill in the blank spaces, increasingly fashioning them into something of greater worth in his kingdom.

The "Michelangelo sermon," as it was commonly called by the research and reflection team, was the second message in the "MasterWorks" series. As shown in Figure 3, the dominant metaphor used in the sermon was a sculpted masterpiece, more particularly, Michelangelo's famous *Pietà* located at Saint Peter's Basilica in Rome, Italy.

The sermon was titled "The Maker's Mark" and grew out of Luke 2:25-35 where Mary and Joseph travel to Jerusalem where they ceremonially present their young son to God in keeping with Jewish law:

> Now there was a man in Jerusalem called Simeon, who was righteous and devout. He was waiting for the consolation of Israel, and the Holy Spirit was upon him. It had been revealed to him by the Holy Spirit that he would not die before he had seen the Lord's Christ. Moved by the Spirit, he went into the temple courts. When the parents brought in the child Jesus to do for him what the custom of the Law required, Simeon took him in his arms and praised God, saying:
>
>> "Sovereign Lord, as you have promised,
>> you now dismiss your servant in peace.
>> For my eyes have seen your salvation,
>> which you have prepared in the sight of all people,
>> a light for revelation to the Gentiles
>> and for glory to your temple Israel."

The child's father and mother marveled at what was said about him. Then Simeon blessed them and said to Mary, his mother: "This child is destined to cause the falling and rising of many in Israel, and to be a sign that will be spoken against, so that the thoughts of many hearts will be revealed. And a sword will pierce your own soul too."

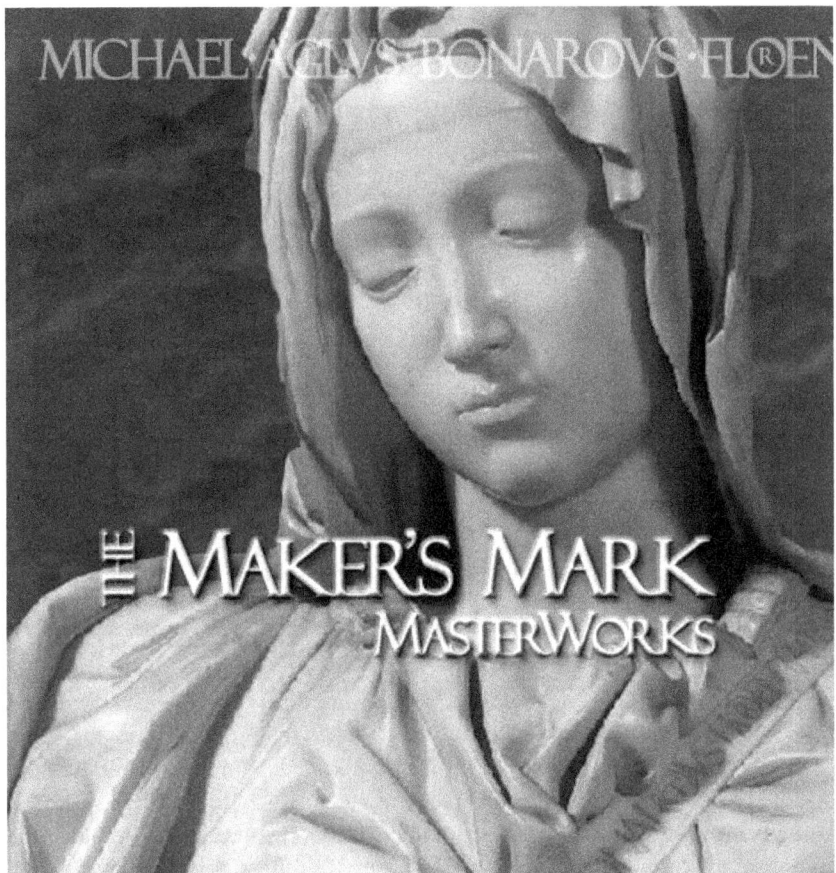

Source: König and Bartz 25

Figure 3. MasterWorks: The Maker's Mark

Luke is the only Gentile in an all-Jewish cast of New Testament writers. In this text he records, from Jesus' earliest days, his mission of including those who were typically treated as outsiders. This child, Jesus, comes to mark both the falling and rising of many in Israel. He will be both misunderstood and contradicted. Even more, Simeon's prophecy cuts like a sharp chisel in the soft marble of the young mother's heart: The joy-filled Mary is warned that a sword will undoubtedly pierce her own soul as well.

The sermon began with an introduction of Michelangelo's *Pietà*. As I described the masterpiece's intricately chiseled features and the talent of its twenty-five year old sculptor, close up, streaming video of the *Pietà* was projected on-screen behind me. Words and images were married from the outset of the sermon. As the camera panned back to reveal less detail and the sculpture's larger context, I shifted from an emphasis on the beauty of Michelangelo's work to the anguish of the scene as Mary cradles her recently crucified Son in her arms. Beauty and pathos were intricately intermingled.

The juxtaposition of these two seemingly contradictory elements introduced the landscape of the sermon text: the holy couple giving thanks to God for their newborn baby Jesus. The setting is a time of great celebration, yet in this case the Scripture paints an ominous shadow of things to come. I invited the congregation to join in brainstorming the many ways joy and angst often come together: "Will my fiancé and I be truly happy?" "Can I really afford to buy a house?" "What if something goes wrong with the baby, or the new job?" Life offers many opportunities for joy and dread, and when the latter comes, everyone is reminded how deeply it cuts.

I shifted gears again, fleshing out Michelangelo's role in the featured metaphor. I offered details about how Michelangelo was commissioned for the work by the elderly French cardinal Jean Bilhères de Lagraulas. I also talked about how, on the cusp of the holy year 1500, the sculpture was installed in the chapel of Santa Petronilla prior to its completion. I shared how Michelangelo continued his work on the sculpture, stupefying large audiences of pilgrims from all over Europe with his amazing skill. Next, I discussed how tradition indicates that one day Michelangelo overheard a conversation by some onlookers in which someone attributed the unsigned sculpture to "our Gobbo from Milan." Soon after the incident, Michelangelo returned to the chapel under the cloak of darkness with hammer and chisel in hand. By the light of a candle, the young sculptor carved his name in beautiful ornate Roman lettering in Latin on the band running diagonally

MICHAEL· AGLVS· BONAROVS· FLOENT· FACEBAT

across the Virgin's chest (see Figure 4).

Figure 4. *Pietà* Inscription: Michelangelo Buonarroti From Florence Made This

Once more, the sermon weaved its way back again to the congregation's connection with the very human Mary of Scripture. Rather than serving primarily as a message giver and problem solver, I was now a fellow journeyman:

> Who could fault Michelangelo? What parents haven't rightfully taken pride in their children? "He has his mother's eyes," a baby's proud father beams. Yet, even the proudest parents must ultimately admit the limitations of their own creativity ability. Which of us can cradle a newborn baby without recognizing the Creator's divine spark that brings vibrancy and life to our DNA?

With the congregation now sharing in Mary's joy, I continued:

> But who hasn't also experienced the pain of loss, the bitter pill of tragedy? And which of us hasn't thought at some point in a moment of joy: remember this moment when trouble comes around again? Joy and sorrow are intricately woven together.

Sooner or later, when the unspeakable spears of life cut so deeply, I illustrated how our anguish will find its home in one of two places:

We can fester bitterly in our agony or we can bring our pain to the Incarnate God who intimately knows our suffering. In the first case, we join the likes of Michelangelo by branding our names across our own hearts. As masters of our destiny, we often cause the pain we own as we chisel our own name over our hearts. At moments like this, our tenacious grip only makes matters worse. The end result: we are pocked with destructive hammer blows not too far removed from what happened to the *Pietà* on Pentecost Sunday 1972. Lurking within a crowd of pilgrims, Laszlo Toth, a thirty-three year-old Australian geologist, dashed past Vatican guards, vaulted a marble balustrade, and attacked Michelangelo's sculpture with a sledgehammer, shouting "I am Jesus Christ!" With fifteen blows, Toth removed the Virgin's arm at the elbow, knocked off a chunk of her nose, and chipped one of her eyelids.

At this point in the sermon, the graphic shown in Figure 5 was projected behind me. "So whose name is carved over your heart? Will you bear the mark of your Maker?" I asked rhetorically. Finally, in talking about the tendency human beings have of placing their own names over their hearts, I shared that our consolation only comes as we allow God's name to be inscribed over our hearts.

In this sermon, the congregation was challenged to recognize God's place in all of life's joys and sorrows. Through visual and verbal cues, the gospel honestly offering recovery to the congregation while at the same time exposing failure, ultimately revealing not only who they really were but also who they could become in Christ.

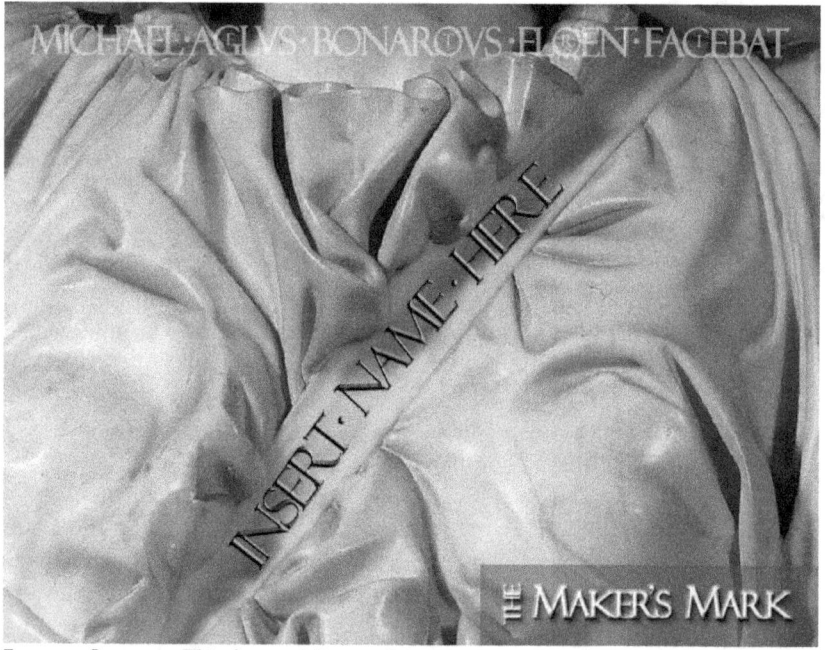

Image Source: König and Bartz 25

Figure 5. Insert Name Here

Conclusion

Through an examination of biblical and theological precedents, preachers have much to learn not only from Jesus, but also from the historic expanse of both testaments. The traditions of the Church, growing out of the collective experience of God's people across the ages, offer great wisdom for those who seek to creatively communicate the compelling message of God. The ebb and flow of history reveal how the Church has wrestled with the place of imagery as a communicative form. The twenty-first-century preacher joins in this challenge. Given the growing number of people who prefer to gain access to information through more interactive means, and after considering the impact of visual media in preaching, preachers are wise to broaden their communication repertoire and, in the process, offer more concrete ways of engaging worshipers in the warp and woof of Scripture.

CHAPTER THREE

DESIGN OF THE STUDY

Building on a review of the literature as outlined in the previous chapter and framed within the context of my own ministry at New Hope Community Church of the Nazarene in Tempe, Arizona, the third chapter of this study focuses particularly on the design of the study and its use in applying the research to preaching to a congregation of multiple generations in an emerging postmodern age. This dissertation is a correlational study examining the relationship between congregational assessments regarding the use of visual media in preaching and respondents' dogmatism and personal orientation toward postmodernism.

Problem and Purpose

The purpose of the study is to determine which factors relate to the use of visual media in preaching in an emerging postmodern cultural context.

Hypothesis

This study seeks to discern if receptivity to the use of visual media in preaching is generationally related and if it is more dominant in those who embrace postmodern cultural values and postliterate characteristics.

Research Questions

The following research questions provided the framework for this dissertation.

Research Question #1

How open or closed to change are survey respondents based on their responses to the Modified Rokeach E? The answer to this question provided a baseline for the comparison with respondents' dogmatism scores with their own orientation toward postmodernism.

Research Question #2

To what degree are survey respondents either modern or postmodern in their orientation to culture? I hypothesize that postmodern cultural values are becoming transgenerational while recognizing that they are likely more dominant among younger adults who have been immersed in them. This research question sought to discern the degree to which all respondents embrace the postmodern cultural values of subjective experience, disillusionment, diversity, and the influence of media.

Research Question #3

How receptive are survey respondents to the use of visual media in preaching? This research question sought to determine the degree to which respondents embrace the use of visual media in preaching. At the beginning of my ministry at New Hope, I presumed that younger people preferred the use of visual media in preaching, while older individuals generally would not.

Research Question #4

To what extent are respondents postliterate and how does postliteracy relate to their receptivity to the use of visual media in preaching? This research question endeavored to determine respondent preferences for textual or visual information through preferred media sources and memory triggers in everyday life as well as in relation to sermon retention.

Research Question #5

What other variables might correlate with participant responses to the use of visual media in preaching? The final research question considers other possible variables, such as gender and other demographic questions compared with the Modified Rokeach E and other survey questions.

Research Methodology

The research project was an evaluative study in the nonexperimental mode utilizing a quantitative cross-sectional survey. I did not use a comparison group outside the church to evaluate the use of visual media in preaching at New Hope. Since I had been using visual media in my preaching at New Hope for more than four years, a cross-sectional design was necessary because a baseline was no longer available.

Population and Sample

The population for this study consisted of worshipers, age 14 and older, at New Hope Community Church of the Nazarene in Tempe, Arizona. Given the cross-sectional design of this quantitative study, participants were not required to attend the church for a specific number of weeks prior to completion of the survey. The treatment of exposure to visual media in preaching varied depending on a person's experience and history at New Hope.

The population and sample were identical for this study; every volunteer age fourteen and older in attendance on Sunday, 21 September was included in the study. The participants (n=104) were either members or attenders at New Hope, and no participants were excluded provided they met the minimum age requirement of 14 years of age. Minors between the ages of 14 and 17 were permitted to complete the survey instrument provided a parent signed a consent form (see Appendix D).

Variables

Using a correlational study in the nonexperimental mode, I examined the relationships between a number of variables incorporated in the researcher-designed questionnaire. These variables included the degree to which respondents were dogmatic according to the Modified Rokeach E, their receptivity to the use of visual media in preaching, and the degrees to which respondents viewed themselves as both postmodern and postliterate. A number of other demographic variables were included in the study, including age, gender, church experience, church affiliation, and tenure at New Hope.

Instrumentation

The research instrument utilized in this study was designed by the researcher and incorporated a standardized dogmatism scale. It was presented to respondents in booklet format and consisted of a cover letter and four sections that are outlined as follows. Each section of the research instrument is provided in Appendix A.

Cover Letter. The cover letter introduced respondents to the survey in general. A primary purpose of the cover letter also centered on its goal of encouraging respondent participation. The cover letter indicated that the study met part of my doctor of ministry requirements at Asbury Theological Seminary and specified that submission of the survey indicated the respondent's consent to participate in the study. Personally signed by me, the cover letter personally expressed appreciation to every volunteer who was willing to take part in the survey research. Within the instrument itself, the cover letter was not given a section number. However, its role in soliciting respondent participation was essential.

Section 1: Demographic information. The first section of the study included some demographic information in the form of five selected-response questions. These multiple-choice items in the researcher-designed survey included details such as gender, age category, respondents' relationship with God, and attendance at New Hope Church. In addition, three hypothetical questions that called for respondents to indicate their preferences for either text or imagery were included in this section. While these three questions were not demographic in nature, these questions were included at the end of the first section because they matched the format of the other questions. Readability of the survey was enhanced by including these questions in this section rather than with the other media-related questions, which utilized a seven-point Likert scale in the third section of the study.

Section 2: The Modified Rokeach Dogmatism Scale (E). The second section of the research instrument measured dogmatism or a respondent's natural receptivity to change. This section of the study measured a respondent's relative openness or closedness to change by utilizing a shortened form of the Dogmatism Scale developed by Milton Rokeach. Originally, Rokeach designed his Form A instrument with fifty-seven items (Hill 490). He came to his final Form E in 1960 after four revisions utilizing eighty-nine different items (Hill 490). Earlier versions of Rokeach's scale, which go back to 1952, contain as many as sixty-eight questions (Hill 490). Rokeach E utilized forty items and was designed for administration in the United States. This study employed a twenty-item scale proposed by Verling Troldahl and Frederic Powell, which had been condensed from Rokeach E.

A modified version was used as a foundational element in the study because Rokeach E has been tested extensively since its inception in 1960. Furthermore, Rokeach E sets out to assess a person's general intolerance, which can be helpful when comparing responses to the more tolerant qualities often exemplified by postmodern individuals. Rokeach E is designed to measure any kind of dogmatism, rather than religious dogmatism only, and strives to measure a respondent's general belief system rather than the specific content of his or her beliefs. Peter Hill indicates that according to Rokeach, "people with closed belief systems are classified as dogmatic. They are characterized by viewing authority as absolute" (490). Hill explains further:

> A person with a closed belief system is quick to reject any opinions or ideas that conflict with his or her accepted view. Such individuals

tend to compartmentalize their beliefs in such a way that conflicting concepts from different sources of authority can exist in relative isolation from each other and therefore remain unscrutinized by the believer. (490)

By the same token, individuals who are less dogmatic on the Rokeach E are prone to assess information from authority figures in combination with material from other sources. Less dogmatic people have more open belief systems and are willing to consider perspectives other than their own. Hill observes that "[c]onflicting concepts are not kept in isolation from one another but are tested through application to resolve discrepancies. The open person does not understand the world as threatening" (490). For Rokeach, the primary distinction between open and closed belief systems is the degree to which individuals rely on absolute authority.

Rokeach E was originally developed for use as a self-administered test but was adapted for use in personal interviews as well. This study followed the original design as a self-administered test because individual reliability coefficients for interviewing ranged only from .30 to .59 while the range on self-administered scales ranged from .35 to .73.

One problem with Rokeach E was the length of the primary measuring instrument. Since the context for the survey immediately followed a Sunday morning worship service, I was concerned that Rokeach E was too time-consuming to fit the design of the study. On average, the research literature indicated that researchers should allow roughly twenty minutes to administer all forty questions in Rokeach E (Hill 490). Since the scale was roughly one-quarter of this study's entire research instrument, and because the data collection was scheduled to take place at the end of a Sunday morning worship service, I sought a shortened form of Rokeach's instrument.

A review of the literature revealed two primary short forms of Rokeach E for use with adults. In 1963, Rolf Schulze tested college students in his research using a ten-item short form of Rokeach E. Julian Biggers indicated that the ten-item Schulze scale had an estimated overall reliability of .62 (10), compared with Rokeach's own reported range of reliability coefficients from .68 to .93 on Form E (Hill 490). The low reliability of Schulze's short form necessitated a further search for a short, yet still reliable, form of the forty-item Rokeach E.

Verling Troldahl and Frederic Powell's twenty-item short form of Rokeach's instrument was introduced in 1965. While Schulze worked with college students, Troldahl and Powell surveyed adults in Lansing, Michigan, and Boston, Massachusetts. Troldahl and Powell fared better than Schulze, obtaining an estimated reliability of .79 for their twenty-item scale (Biggers 10). They offer their conclusions about the propriety of using a shorter form of Rokeach's instrument:

> It would seem that the 20-item version could be used without much reluctance. Its reliability is at about the minimum desired by most researchers. Ten or 15 item versions should probably be used only if the researcher feels he needs a gross index of dogmatism or is willing to use one for economic reasons. If he uses these earlier versions, he should be aware that the relationships he finds between dogmatism and other variables will be lower than he would have obtained if he had used a more precise measure of dogmatism, because of chance error in his dogmatism scores. (Troldahl and Powell 214)

Respondents were asked to indicate their relative agreement or disagreement to all twenty questions in the Troldahl-Powell short form. No items in the shortened version were negatively worded. For continuity, all questions in this section and the two sections that followed were structured on seven-point Likert scales. Two questions were reworded to make them more culturally relevant. Q2A, which originally read, "The United States and Russia have just about nothing in common," was replaced with "The United States and Iraq have just about nothing in common," to account for current world events. Q2P, which originally read, "Most of the ideas that get printed nowadays aren't worth the paper they are printed on," was reworded slightly as follows: "Most of the ideas that get published today aren't worth the paper they are printed on." This modification sought to include more contemporary language while still retaining the original context of the question in relation to a print-dominant world. The range of scores for the short form is 20 to 140, with a high score indicating the respondent is dogmatic and more prone to have a closed belief system.

Troldahl and Powell's twenty-item short form of the Rokeach E was incorporated into this research study because it offered better reliability than the Schulze ten-item scale and it could be administered on a Sunday morning after church in less time than the original Rokeach E survey instrument.

Section 3: Media questionnaire. Having used visual media in my preaching at New Hope for over four years, I was already familiar with many of the arguments used by those who oppose the practice. Several of the questions in section three grew directly out of conversations I have had with those who oppose the use of visual media in preaching.

The third section of the research instrument centered on eleven statements arranged on seven-point Likert scales. The survey asked respondents to indicate the degree to which they agreed or disagreed with each statement. Questions A, E, F, G, and I were negatively worded in support of the modern view; the remaining questions were designed to find support by postmodern individuals. The face validity of the survey questions was supported in the pretest by the lack of any apparent confusion on the part of any of the pretest respondents.

Section 4: Postmodern values questionnaire. As stated previously, individuals who embrace postmodern cultural characteristics often exhibit an inherent disinclination toward categorization. This personal trait, influenced by culture, can make a researcher's task even more difficult in a study like this one. While postmodern people exhibit a wide variety of personal beliefs, this cross-sectional quantitative survey identified five cultural values often embraced by postmodern individuals. I asked respondents to indicate their relative agreement or disagreement to each one on seven-point Likert scales. Survey questions were designed personally or adapted from either Huckins' nonstandardized Postmodern Identification Questionnaire (see Appendix B) or the nonstandardized Steele-Drovdahl-Grenz Postmodern Survey (see Appendix C). Questions A, B, C, F, N, and O in this section were negatively worded to embrace a more modern worldview. The remaining ten questions were worded to affirm the postmodern vantage point. The distribution of these cultural values across the spectrum of all sixteen questions for this section is defined in Table 4.

Table 4. Key to Postmodern Values Questionnaire

Postmodern Cultural Values	Reference Questions in Section 4
Community	D, G
Disillusionment	C, N
Diversity	K
Subjective Experience	A, B, E, I, J, L, O
Influence of Media	F, H, M, P

Pilot Testing

On Sunday, 24 August 2003 the instrument was pilot tested by the five following volunteer members of the Research and Reflection Team: Glenn Chaffee, Darlene Coleman, Marilee Naeve, Barbara Schumacher, and Margie Shannon. The questionnaire was completed by one person in approximately twenty minutes; the other four respondents completed the survey in eleven to twelve minutes. Pilot test respondents were also encouraged to consider layout, sentence structure, and overall readability in addition to taking the test itself. The questionnaire was also reviewed by Dr. William Brown, a professor at Arizona State University, who is also a member of the research and reflection team. Comments from the respondents centered primarily on the wording of a few questions and also encouraged me to introduce each section of the survey more clearly. Since most of the suggestions regarding the instrument's format were minor, a second test of the survey was not necessary.

Data Collection

Prior to the day of data collection, I invited the congregation to attend New

Hope on Sunday, 21 September 2003 in order to take part in the study. I clearly indicated that the study was voluntary and that it partially fulfilled the requirements for my completion of the doctor of ministry degree at Asbury Theological Seminary.

Following the worship service at New Hope on Sunday, 21 September, worshipers were encouraged to remain after the service to complete the survey. Of the 129 people in attendance that day, 77 of them were fourteen or older and all chose to voluntarily take part in the survey. Parents of respondents under the age of 18 were required to sign a Parental Consent Form (see Appendix D). Due to scheduling conflicts, many other individuals meeting the above criteria asked to complete the survey after the primary date of data collection. I also made large print copies of the survey instrument available to anyone requesting one. Four individuals took advantage of the large print surveys on the primary day of data collection. A total of 113 respondents completed the survey instrument.

After giving an overview of general instructions and several references to the material on the cover letter, I emphasized confidentiality and the need for honest responses. Survey participants took between nine and seventeen minutes to complete the survey, with most people spending roughly twelve minutes on it. Members of the research and reflection team distributed the surveys and were available at both exits at the conclusion of the testing period to direct respondents to place their completed surveys in the church's offering basket.

Data Analysis

The survey data were analyzed by the *Statistical Package for the Social Sciences* software (*SPSS*). Immediately following the data collection, the survey data were entered from each survey into an *Excel* spreadsheet (*Microsoft*). This information was then imported into the SPSS statistical package. Those who completed large print surveys were safeguarded from identification by having their anonymous survey data transferred by an impartial volunteer onto standard sized surveys. These surveys were then randomly shuffled into the mix with the other surveys prior to data entry. Negatively worded items were reverse scored in SPSS to correspond with positively worded items in each corresponding scale.

Analysis began with an examination of frequencies within the demographic material in the first section of the survey, followed by reliability analyses for sections two through four of the instrument. In some cases, Varimax rotations were used to identify statistically identifiable factors within particular scales. Crosstabs, Pearson Correlations, analyses of variance (ANOVA), regression analyses, and comparisons of group means by t-tests were also used in the analysis phase. The data were reported in a descriptive manner.

CHAPTER FOUR

FINDINGS OF THE STUDY

The purpose of this study was to determine which factors related to a person's receptiveness toward visual media in preaching. Given my pastoral experience at New Hope Church prior to the project, I did not see any clear correlation between congregant age and media receptivity. This discovery is noteworthy because I adopted a popular hypothesis during my doctor of ministry coursework at Asbury, namely, that Baby Busters, raised in the emerging postmodern culture with a steady diet of television and electronic media, would be more receptive to things visual than their older counterparts. This chapter provides a profile of respondent answers and relates the research findings to the five research questions outlined in Chapter 3.

Respondent Profiles

To ensure the likelihood of every respondent's anonymity at New Hope Church, this study limited personal identifying information to five demographic questions outlined earlier in Chapter 3. Of the 113 people who completed the survey instrument, 54 percent (n=61) were women, and 46 percent (n=52) were men. The research instrument asked respondents to identify their age according to the same five-item generational scale shown in Table 1 (see p. 22). Only one respondent declined to answer the question which asked, "When were you born?" The demographic distribution for these five generational groupings is shown in Table 5. Since only four respondents were born prior to 1925, I merged the Senior respondents with the slightly younger Builder generation who were born between 1925-44. By merging the survey information from Seniors, they could still be analyzed as part of a larger body of data by accommodating for slightly broader age characteristics. From this point forward, Seniors and Builders were combined as one demographic group for the remainder of the study.

Table 5. Modified Respondent Age (N=113)

Q1B - When were you born?	n	%
Before 1944	14	12.4
Between 1945-63	50	44.2
1964-80	35	31.0
After 1980	13	11.5
No Response	1	0.9

With regard to respondents' relationship with God, 78.8 percent of survey participants (n=89) indicated that they made a commitment to Christ prior to attending New Hope Church. Those who committed their lives to Christ after attending New Hope amounted to 17.7 percent of all respondents (n=20). Four respondents were unsure about their relationship with God, and no respondents indicated they had not yet made a commitment to Christ.

The fourth demographic question within Section One related to tenure at New Hope Church. The data indicate that slightly more than one in five respondents began attending New Hope in the past year (n=24). On the other side of the spectrum, nearly half of the respondents (n=55) attended the church for some time prior to my arrival as pastor in 1999. Table 6 indicates that while one respondent failed to answer the question, two groups dominated the sample: those who began attending New Hope Church prior to my arrival (n=55) and a total of those who came afterward (n= 57). These two groups of near identical size were, therefore, used as distinct demographic groups for all subsequent assessments in reference to congregational tenure.

Table 6. Respondent Tenure at New Hope Church (N=113)

Q1D – How long have you attended New Hope?	n	%
First-time guest	3	2.7
Less than a month	4	3.5
One to six months	8	7.1
Six months to one year	9	8.0
One to four years	33	29.2
Prior to Pastor Akkerman's arrival in 1999	55	48.7
No Response	1	.9

The final demographic question asked respondents to describe their attendance at New Hope Church for the previous six months. This question specified New Hope as the attendance venue given the church's use of visual media in preaching and its centrality to the research study. Nearly 70 percent of the respondents (n=77) self-described their attendance to be nearly every week. Roughly 2 percent of respondents (n=2) did not respond to the question. Table 7 reflects all responses to this survey item.

Table 7. Respondent Attendance at New Hope Church (N=113)

Q1E – Describe your attendance…	n	%
Nearly every week	77	68.1
Twice a month	9	8.0
Once a month	15	13.3
Holidays and special occasions	10	8.8
No Response	2	1.8

Openness to Change

How open or closed to change are survey respondents based on their responses to the Modified Rokeach E?

The first research question related to respondent scores on dogmatism as reflected in the twenty-item scale in Section Two of the research instrument. An analysis of reliability was calculated for every scale in the research instrument, including responses to the dogmatism scale as shown in Table 8. Each of the remaining scales are discussed later in the chapter.

Table 8. Listing of Dissertation Survey Scales (N=113)

Scale	Mean	SD	α
Dogmatism	3.71	.69	.73
Media Scale	5.49	.94	.86
Pastoral Media Subscale	5.97	1.21	.89
Media Imagery Subscale	5.10	.97	.75
Postmodern Values Questionnaire	3.65	.55	.42
Postmodern Subjectivity Subscale	3.83	1.35	.60

The Cronbach alpha is a tool for assessing the internal reliability or consistency within a statistical scale and is helpful in determining the degree to which a scale measures a single construct. Items within a scale that correlate well with each other indicate they are measuring the same underlying construct. In these cases, Cronbach alpha increases. By the same token, a scale made up of a wide variety of constructs will result in a low inter-item correlation, reflecting a correspondingly low Cronbach alpha score. A reliability coefficient of .70 or greater is considered acceptable in social science applications.

Section Two of the survey resulted in a Cronbach alpha score of .73, which is slightly lower than Troldahl and Powell's estimated reliability of .79 for the same twenty-item scale (Biggers 10). By the same token, dogmatism fell between Rokeach's own reported range of reliability coefficients from .68 to .93 on Form E (Hill 490). The alpha coefficient for dogmatism was within the accepted range for social science research applications of this type.

The mean score for all respondents (n=113) on dogmatism was 3.71 (SD=.69). Using a seven-point Likert scale, this placed the average for all respondents roughly in the middle of the continuum, indicating they were moderately dogmatic.

I was especially interested in the degree to which each generational group scored on dogmatism. Prior to the study, I hypothesized that younger respondents would likely score less dogmatic than older ones. This assumption bore out statistically with one exception. As a whole, Seniors and Builders (mean=3.93; SD=.78) were more dogmatic than Baby Boomers (mean=3.60; SD=.72). Likewise, Baby Boomers were, in turn, slightly more dogmatic than Baby Busters (mean=3.59; SD=.58). However, with respect to the Millenialists, the survey data revealed the opposite: this youngest generational group, who were born after 1980, scored higher on dogmatism than any other group with a mean score of 4.05 (SD=.49) on a seven-point scale. Standard deviations for the four generational groups increased from .49 with Millenialists to .78 with Seniors and Builders, indicating a tighter cluster of similar scores by younger respondents and a wider disparity of responses as age increased by generational group. Table 9 reports the research findings in greater detail.

Table 9. Dogmatism Scores by Generational Group (N=112)

Generational Group	N	Mean	SD
Seniors and Builders	14	3.93	.78
Baby Boomers	50	3.60	.72
Baby Busters	35	3.59	.58
Millennialists	13	4.05	.49

An analysis of variance (ANOVA) was calculated to examine the statistical differences between the means of all four generational groups. The relationship between the mean and the likelihood of random error for each group indicates whether the difference between the two is statistically significant or not. An analysis of dogmatism between age groupings revealed no statistically significant difference between mean scores.

Postmodernism

To what degree are survey respondents either modern or postmodern in their orientation to culture?

Given the natural disinclination of postmodern women and men to be categorized, the second research question was the most difficult one to assess. I hoped that the adapted sixteen-item scale used in Section Four of the research instrument would prove helpful in this respect, particularly since it included a number of questions by Dr. Stanley Grenz, who is regarded as an expert on postmodernism.

Section Four sought to examine the five following constructs within postmodernism: community, disillusionment, diversity, subjective experience, and influence of media. This sixteen-item scale was developed from a collection of researcher-designed questions as well as those from two nonstandardized research instruments referred to in this study as the Huckins Postmodern Identification Scale and the Steele-Drovdahl-Grenz Postmodernism Survey (see Appendixes B and C).

The Cronbach alpha for Section Four of the research instrument indicated a reliability coefficient of only .42 for the sixteen-item scale (see Table 8). This alpha is far below the acceptable standard of .70 in social science research. As a result, the questions in this scale were deemed unreliable for analysis. A factor analysis using a Varimax rotation of the same sixteen items resulted in seven factors with Eigen values greater than 1.00. The strongest of these factors consisted of three questions that are shown in Table 10. This factor became a subscale that accounted for 14 percent of the variance in all sixteen questions within the larger scale. None of the other six factors resulted in a reliable subscale. The three questions in this factor became known as the Postmodern Subjectivity Subscale and are delineated in Table 10.

Table 10. Postmodern Subjectivity Subscale (N=113)

Question		Factor Loading
Q4E	Truth can vary based on the individual.	.74
Q4I	It is difficult to be certain about much of anything today.	.62
Q4L	I prefer to say that something is "appropriate" rather than if it is "right."	.74

A reliability analysis for the Postmodern Subjectivity Subscale resulted in a Cronbach alpha of .60. Clearly, this reliability coefficient is less than the acceptable minimum of .70, but it is considerably better than the overall alpha of .42 for Section Four of the research instrument as a whole. For purposes of assessment, the Postmodern Subjectivity Subscale was utilized in this study to address the second research question and examine correlating factors leading to respondent receptivity toward the use of electronic visual media in preaching.

The mean score for all respondents (n=113) on the Postmodern Subjectivity Subscale was 3.83 (SD=1.35). Using a seven-point Likert scale, this placed the average for all respondents very near the center of the range. Since the majority of respondents (n=64) were either Seniors, Builders, or Baby Boomers, many would suspect that the Postmodern Subjectivity Subscale would be lower; however, the data indicate that the postmodern trait of subjectivity was exhibited in each generational group surveyed (see Table 11). In fact, the data showed that the oldest group in the research study also scored highest on the Postmodern Subjectivity Subscale with a mean of 4.40 (SD=1.39). The data revealed no significant difference of mean scores between groups, based on both age and gender.

Table 11. Postmodern Subjectivity Subscale Scores by Generational Group (N=112)

Generational Group	n	Mean	SD
Seniors and Builders	14	4.40	1.39
Baby Boomers	50	3.77	1.39
Baby Busters	35	3.57	1.32
Millennialists	13	4.05	1.15

Media Receptivity

How receptive are survey respondents to the use of visual media in preaching?

The third research question considered the degree to which survey respondents were receptive to the use of visual media in preaching. During my residency in the Beeson program, I assumed that younger worship participants would likely be more receptive than older ones toward the use of visual media in preaching. However, congregational growth across all age groupings at New Hope Church caused me to reconsider this assumption; this discovery later served as a catalyst for this research study.

Section Three of the survey instrument was comprised of eleven researcher-designed questions relating to respondents' personal beliefs and observations of the use of visual media specifically at New Hope Church. A reliability analysis of the questions in this section of the survey revealed that this scale maintained the highest inter-item reliability of any in the instrument, with a Cronbach alpha of .86.

The mean score for all respondents (n=113) on the Media Scale was 5.49 (SD=.94). Using a seven-point Likert scale, this score placed the average for all respondents on the high side of the continuum. Table 12 offers a more detailed breakdown based on generational grouping. To some extent, I was not surprised since many respondents in the congregation had been exposed to my use of visual media in preaching for over four years at the time of the cross-sectional research study.

Table 12. Media Scale Scores by Generation (N=112)

Generational Group	n	Mean	SD
Seniors and Builders	14	5.31	1.32
Baby Boomers	50	5.50	1.00
Baby Busters	35	5.55	.76
Millennialists	13	5.52	.68

An interesting discovery came when comparing the Media Scale with those who had either made a commitment to Christ before or after attending New Hope Church. Those who indicated their commitment to Christ prior to attending New Hope scored a mean of 5.37 (SD=.98) on the Media Scale while those who made a commitment to Christ subsequent to arriving at the church scored a mean of 6.01 (SD=.49). A much lower standard deviation on the part of the second group indicates that responses were clustered more closely together than they were for those who came to New Hope after accepting Christ. A t-test for equality of means between both groups revealed a two-tailed significance (t=-2.80; df=107; p$\leq$.01). By the same token, an ANOVA comparing mean scores revealed that the relationship between generational grouping and Media Scale scores was not significant.

Media Subscales

After entering all eleven questions from the Media Scale into a factor analysis using a Varimax rotation, I identified two distinct factors, each with a high degree of inter-item reliability and Eigen values in excess of 1.00. The first factor, hereafter known as the Pastoral Media Subscale (□ =.89), accounted for 47 percent of the variance. The second factor became known as the Media Imagery Subscale (α=.75) for the remainder of the data analysis. The second subscale accounted for 14 percent of the variance on the larger Media Scale.

Pastoral Media Subscale. Comprised of five items from the Media Scale, the Pastoral Media Subscale had a Cronbach alpha of .89. All five items were worded negatively and were reverse scored. After recoding, a higher score on this subscale reflected higher respondent receptivity to the pastor's use of media. Each item in the subscale related either directly or indirectly to me as pastor and, more specifically, to my use of visual media in preaching at New Hope Church. Table 13 outlines the five questions that made up the Pastoral Media Subscale and includes their individual factor loads.

Table 13. Pastoral Media Subscale (N=112)

Question		Factor Loading
Q3E	Generally, I find the pastor's use of visual media distracting.	.85
Q3F	Using visual media in preaching today is a gimmick.	.86
Q3G	I suspect the pastor likely chooses video clips <u>before</u> selecting his Bible text.	.75
Q3I	Often, the visual media used in the sermon do <u>not</u> relate to the Bible text.	.80
Q3K	I wish the pastor would stop using visual media in his preaching.	.84

Note: All items in this subscale were reverse scored in SPSS

The mean score for all respondents (n=113) on the Pastoral Media Subscale was 5.97 (SD=1.21). Using a seven-point Likert scale, the average for all respondents was quite high on the continuum. In fact, the mean for this subscale was the highest of any in the research study. A *t*-test revealed no statistically significant difference between the mean scores based on gender.

With respect to those who made commitments to Christ prior or subsequent to their attendance at New Hope, the survey data revealed that those who made a prior Christian commitment (n=89) scored 5.87 (SD=1.28) on the Pastoral Media Subscale, while those who committed themselves to Christ following their attendance at New Hope (n=20) scored 6.44 (SD=.53) on the same subscale. Individuals were more likely to score higher on the Media Scale if they also made a Christian commitment at the church. Likewise, the standard deviation for those who made a commitment to Christ at New Hope was considerably lower (SD=.53) than it was for those who made a prior commitment (SD=1.28), which indicates that the prior group tended to score more tightly in a cluster than the latter group. A t-test for equality of means between both groups revealed a two-tailed significance (t=-1.97; df=107; p$\leq$.05).

The correlation analysis shown in Table 14 details the Cronbach alpha for each scale and describes the relationship between each variable. Regarding the Postmodern Subjectivity Subscale, Table 14 indicates that no statistically significant relationships exist between it and the other scales. Not surprisingly, a statistically significant relationship exists between the Media Scale and both the Pastoral Media Subscale and the Media Imagery Subscale. This is not noteworthy because the subscales come from the Media Imagery Scale. Likewise, the statistically significant relationship between the Pastoral Media Subscale and the Media Imagery Subscale are not noteworthy since both are closely related to the same construct. However, the analysis did reveal a statistically significant negative correlation between dogmatism and the Pastoral Media Subscale (r=-.22; p$\leq$.05). In other words, the analysis revealed that those who scored low on dogmatism tended to score higher on the Pastoral Media Subscale. Respondents who tended to be more open to change also tended to indicate a higher level of receptivity to the pastor and his use of visual media in preaching. Likewise, those who were more dogmatic were also more likely to score lower on the Pastoral Media Subscale. This discovery indicates that those who were more closed to change were also more likely to negatively score those questions that related to me as a preacher and my use of visual media in preaching at New Hope Church. Since the Pastoral Media Subscale pertains to respondent attitudes specifically toward me as their pastor and my use of visual media in preaching at New Hope Church, it is an important tool for analysis in this study.

Table 14. Correlation of Variables in Analysis

Scale	1	2	3	4	5
1. Postmodern Subjectivity Subscale	(.60)				
2. Dogmatism	.03	(.73)			
3. Media Scale	.11	-.13	(.86)		
4. Pastoral Media Subscale	.05	-.22*	.88**	(.89)	
5. Media Imagery Subscale	.14	-.01	.87**	.52**	(.75)

Note: Values in parentheses are alpha coefficients for measurement scales;

$n=113$; *$p \leq .05$, **$p \leq .01$, ***$p \leq .001$

Media Imagery Subscale. This subscale is made up of six items from the Media Scale that all relate to respondent attitudes toward the use of visual media in preaching. A reliability analysis on the Media Imagery Subscale revealed a Cronbach alpha of .75 (n=113). Table 15 delineates each item within the subscale along with the corresponding factor loadings. The first item in the scale was reverse scored in SPSS, meaning that those who rated themselves high on this item tended to be textually oriented rather than visually oriented.

Table 15. Media Imagery Subscale (N=112)

Question		Factor Loading
Q3A	Images are nice in sermons, but words really get the point across to me.	.73
Q3B	A picture really is worth a thousand words, even in a sermon.	.68
Q3C	I have been emotionally moved by the use of visual media in a sermon.	.62
Q3D	Jesus used the visual methods of his day in his communication.	.47
Q3H	My friends would likely find our church's use of visual media interesting.	.67
Q3J	I like visual media because it is easier for me to see the screen than to read.	.60

Note: Q3A in this subscale was reverse scored in SPSS

The mean score for all respondents (n=113) on the Media Imagery Subscale was 5.10 (SD=.97). Using a seven-point Likert scale, the average for all respondents was high on the continuum and was consistent with the other two media-related scales in the study. A *t*-test revealed no statistically significant difference between the mean scores based on gender.

Research Question #4

To what extent are respondents postliterate and how does postliteracy relate to their receptivity to the use of visual media in preaching?

The final three questions in Section One of the research instrument sought to determine respondent preferences toward either literacy or postliteracy. One question asked respondents to imagine themselves locating friends from school days in an old yearbook. Respondents were given a choice between two hypothetical options: an image-based postliterate option that involved looking at yearbook photos to trigger their memory, or a textually based literate option that involved scanning a list of names in the yearbook as a memory trigger. In every case, generational groups overwhelmingly preferred image-based memory triggers rather than textually based ones. A crosstab was processed for this question to define individual responses by generational grouping (see Table 16). Approximately three-quarters of all respondents (n=85) self-described themselves as preferring image-based triggers, regardless of age. Age was not a determining factor of whether people preferred image-based or textually based memory triggers and the data were not statistically significant.

Table 16. Crosstab on Memory Triggers (N=111)

Generational Group	Text n	Image n
Builders and Seniors	6	7
Baby Boomers	13	37
Baby Busters	6	29
Millenialists	1	12

A t-test was conducted to compare memory trigger responses with scores on both the Media Scale and the Pastoral Media Subscale. The mean score on the Media Scale was 5.62 (SD=.84) for those who preferred image-based memory triggers (n=85) compared to those with textually based memory triggers (n=26) who scored 5.06 on the mean (SD=1.12). The t-test revealed a two-tailed significance (t=2.81; df=110; p$\leq$.01). On the Pastoral Media Subscale, those who preferred image-based memory triggers scored a mean of 6.12 (SD=1.11) compared with those who had textually based triggers with a mean score of 5.50 (SD=1.42). The t-test for this second comparison of means indicated a two-tailed significance as well (t=2.32; df=110; p$\leq$.05).

Finally, a comparison of means was conducted on the Media Imagery Subscale, indicating a mean of 5.22 (SD=.91) for those with image triggers and 4.69 (SD=1.07) for those with textual triggers. A t-test for equality of means likewise revealed a two-tailed significance on the final subscale (t=2.54; df=110; p$\leq$.01). Clearly, those with image-based memory triggers are more receptive to the use of visual media in preaching than those with textually based ones.

The second item relating to postliteracy asked respondents to identify their preferred media form for news: newspapers, radio, television, and the Internet were the forced choices representing a continuum from literate to postliterate. On the one hand, the research findings for this question shown in Table 17 were not surprising: nearly two-thirds of all respondents (n=70) indicated that television was their preferred media form for news. On the other hand, I was fascinated to discover that Senior and Builder respondents (n=12) were the only generational group to select television unanimously as their preferred news source. As a whole, newspapers ranked last, or at least near the bottom, as respondents' least favorable form of news media. Baby Boomers (n=11) were more inclined to choose the Internet as their primary media form than any other generational group. Nevertheless, Internet users as a whole (n=18) still came in an overwhelmingly distant second to television (n=70). While television is a dominant media form in every generational group, the survey data revealed the lack of a statistically significant relationship between age and news media preference.

Table 17. Crosstab on News Media Preference (N=110)

Generational Group	Newspaper n	Radio n	Television n	Internet n
Builders and Seniors	0	0	12	0
Baby Boomers	5	9	25	11
Baby Busters	4	3	24	4
Millenialists	0	1	9	3

By the same token, I was surprised to find that an expected relationship between dogmatism and preferred news media form did not exist in the survey sample. Prior to the study, I suspected that respondents who scored higher on dogmatism would also be more likely to prefer more traditionally literate news media forms, especially the newspaper. This hypothesis did not bear out statistically. Instead, the data revealed in this instance that dogmatism increased with postliteracy as shown in Table 18. Likewise, standard deviations decreased as respondents chose more postliterate forms of news media. An ANOVA related to dogmatism and news media preference revealed a significant difference between mean scores ($F=3.99$; $df=3,107$; $p\leq.01$).

Table 18. News Media Preference and Dogmatism (N=111)

News Media Preference	Dogmatism		
	N	Mean	SD
Newspaper	9	3.05	.71
Radio	13	3.48	.63
Television	71	3.79	.74
Internet	18	3.83	.26

A t-test for equality of means was also conducted to compare dogmatism and the Media Imagery Subscale on those who self-selected their preferred news media form as newspapers or radio. This test confirmed the ANOVA, revealing that those who preferred television or the Internet ($n=89$) also scored higher (mean=3.80; SD=.67) on dogmatism than those who preferred more literate media forms ($n=22$) like newspaper and radio (mean=3.30; SD=.68). The t-test revealed a two-tailed significance on this comparison ($t=3.11$; $df=109$; $p\leq.01$).

The same t-test also revealed another statistically significant finding: those who preferred television and the Internet also scored higher on the Media Imagery Subscale (mean=5.21; SD=.94). While an ANOVA did not indicate significance as it did in the case above, a t-test revealed a two-tailed significance on this comparison ($t=2.35$; $df=109$; $p\leq.05$). The researcher was not surprised by this finding, confirming a relationship between television and Internet usage and Media Imagery Subscale scores.

I processed another crosstab defining individual responses by generational grouping to the final question in Section One. This question was specific to me and my congregational context at New Hope Church. It asked, "When you think about one of Pastor Jay's past sermons, which are you more likely to remember: stories he told in particular or a visual illustration he used to make his point?" During my residency in the Beeson program, I suspected that younger respondents would more likely be visually oriented than their older counterparts. I presumed that younger respondents would be more likely to retain sermon information on the basis of image rather than story.

This assumption did not appear to bear out in my pastoral assignment and became, in essence, a catalyst for this research project. The crosstab for this question is shown in Table 19. The fairly even distribution of responses in every generational group validates my experience at New Hope rather than my original suspicion at Asbury. It also underscores the importance of context in respect to this question. One question in this section asks a similar question with respect to a more general memory trigger (i.e., visual or textual triggers in a yearbook), but this question sets the context specifically at New Hope Church. As shown previously, 85 out of 111 respondents overwhelmingly supported image triggers over textual ones. With regard to sermon retention, however, responses were more diverse. Slightly more than half of all respondents (n=59) were prone to recall my past sermons by remembering a visual illustration, while 42.5% were more likely to remember a story (n=48). Ironically, in every generational group except the Millenialists, respondents were more likely to remember my past sermons by recalling visual illustrations rather than stories I told in particular. Older respondents did not tend to favor stories over visuals more than any other generational group. The survey data did not support a clear connection between age and sermon retention and the findings were not statistically significant.

Table 19. Crosstab on Sermon Retention (N=107)

Generational Group	Stories n	Visuals n
Builders and Seniors	5	7
Baby Boomers	19	29
Baby Busters	16	18
Millenialists	8	5

I conducted a *t*-test for equality of means based on responses to sermon retention and the Postmodern Subjectivity Subscale, dogmatism, the Pastoral Media Subscale, and the Media Imagery Subscale. This test revealed three statistically significant findings, all of which resulted in negative correlations. First, the data indicated an inverse relationship between Postmodern Subjectivity Subscale scores and respondent preference for textual triggers on sermon retention ($t=-2.81$; $df=105$; $p\leq.01$), which was noteworthy. Second, an inverse relationship also existed between those who scored higher on the Media Scale and respondents' textual trigger preference ($t=-2.83$; $df=105$; $p\leq.01$). Finally, given the previous finding, I was not surprised to learn of an inverse relationship between rankings on the Media Imagery Subscale and respondent preference for textual triggers on sermon retention ($t=-3.05$; $df=105$; $p\leq.01$).

To investigate a possible explanation for the factors leading to receptivity toward visual media, I conducted regression analyses on both the Pastoral Media and the Media Imagery Subscales. In both cases, I controlled these analyses for age.

Pastoral Media Subscale. By excluding selected variables, regression analyses may permit researchers to discover specific influences that contribute to variance in a particular research finding. At times, one influence will dominate an outcome; at other times, a regression analysis reveals multiple influences that contribute to a finding.

With regard to the Pastoral Media Subscale, I conducted a regression analysis controlling for age in reference to the following three variables: dogmatism, sermon retention, and the Postmodern Subjectivity Subscale. Using the stepwise regression feature, dogmatism was selected as a contributing factor in step two. This factor accounted for 11 percent of the variance in the Pastoral Media Subscale. The third contributing variable entered was a respondent's own preference for sermon retention (i.e., stories or visuals), accounting for 4 percent of the variance in the same subscale. The regression analysis indicated that the Postmodern Subjectivity Subscale did not account for much variance on the Pastoral Media Subscale.

This regression revealed that a respondent's dogmatism contributes more to variance within the Pastoral Media Subscale than any other variable. The degree to which people were postliterate in their retention of sermon information was also a unique contributing factor, although to a lesser degree than dogmatism. Table 20 demonstrates the regression on the Pastoral Media Subscale.

Table 20. Regression on Pastoral Media Subscale

Step	Variable	Beta[a]	T	ΔR²	ΔF
1	Age	.02	.15	.00	.02
2	Dogmatism	-.34	-3.62	.11	13.10***
3	Sermon Retention	.21	2.29	.04	5.25*
$R^2=.16$; F=6.31; df=3,103; $p \leq .001$					

[a]*Standardized Beta for each step, *$p \leq .05$, **$p \leq .01$, ***$p \leq .001$*

Media Imagery Subscale. A regression analysis was also conducted to investigate which factors contributed most to variances within the Media Imagery Subscale. As in the previous analysis, I controlled again for age. Using the stepwise regression feature, sermon retention was selected as a key variable for analysis. The second regression analysis determined no correlation between a respondent's Postmodern Subjectivity Subscale score and his or her ranking on the Media Imagery Subscale. By the same token, a respondent's dogmatism did not account for much variance in the Media Imagery Subscale. Instead, the data indicated that a respondent's preferred method of sermon retention (i.e., literate or postliterate) only accounted for roughly 9 percent of the variance on the Media Imagery Subscale. Apparently, many other factors, yet unknown, account for more variance than whether people tend to remember visual cues. This finding surprised me because I suspected that this factor would have a more direct impact on variance within the subscale. Table 21 illustrates the regression data on the Media Imagery subscale.

Table 21. Regression on Media Imagery Subscale

Step	Variable	Beta[a]	T	ΔR²	ΔF
1	Age	.05	.51	.00	.26
2	Sermon Retention	.30	3.13**	.09	9.80**
R²=.09; F=5.04; df=2,104; p≤.01					

[a]*Standardized Beta for each step, *p≤.05, **p≤.01, ***p≤.001*

Research Question #5

What other variables might correlate with participant responses to the use of visual media in preaching?

The final research question explores which variables, if any, might relate either positively or negatively to respondents' receptivity to the use of visual media in preaching.

Gender

The survey data indicated that women (n=61) scored slightly higher on the Media Scale (mean=5.52; SD=.91) than men (n=52; mean=5.45; SD=.97). On the Pastoral Media Subscale, women (mean=5.98; SD=1.21) also ranked higher than men (mean=5.95; SD=1.21). Likewise, scores from the Media Imagery Subscale indicated that women (mean=5.14; SD=.90) scored higher than men (mean=5.04; SD=1.04). A *t*-test for equality of means by gender revealed that these findings were not statistically significant. Gender did not play a part in respondent receptivity to the use of visual media in preaching.

Attendance

I speculated that those who attended New Hope most regularly would also prefer the use of visual media in preaching more than those who attended less frequently. Not surprisingly, the research data supports this hypothesis.

I calculated an ANOVA comparing mean scores between attendance patterns and the Media Scale (F=5.38; df=3,107; p≤.01), Pastoral Media Subscale (F= 4.49; df=3,107; p≤.01), and Media Imagery Subscale (F=3.22; df=3,107; p≤.05). The ANOVA for these mean scores indicated that all three were statistically significant.

Those who attended New Hope least frequently on holidays or other special occasions (n=10) consistently ranked lowest on the Media Scale with a mean score of 4.52 (SD=1.04), the Pastoral Media Subscale with a mean score of 4.80 (SD=1.61), and the Media Imagery Subscale with a mean score of 4.32 (SD=.98). Not surprisingly, those who indicated their church attendance at nearly every week (n=77) reflected the highest mean scores on all three scales: 5.65 (SD=.81) on the Media Scale; 6.16 (SD=.95) on the Pastoral Media Subscale; and 5.23 (SD=.92) on the Media Imagery Subscale.

Tenure

Prior to the research study, I suspected a relationship between congregant tenure at New Hope and receptivity to visual media, namely, that those who attended New Hope for longer periods of time would tend to be more receptive to the use of visual media in preaching. A *t*-test for equality of means was conducted, which revealed two findings: first, that overall media receptivity was high on the Media Scale, the Pastoral Media Subscale, and the Media Imagery Subscale regardless of respondent tenure based on mean scores; and second, that those who attended New Hope prior to my arrival as pastor preferred visual media in preaching slightly more than those who came after my arrival in 1999 on all three media scales previously mentioned. Nevertheless, the *t*-test also revealed that none of the factors related to these outcomes was statistically significant.

Commitment

I was also interested to learn whether a correlation existed between receptivity to visual media in preaching and the timing of a congregant's commitment to Christ. In other words, were people who had made a commitment to Christ prior to attending New Hope any less receptive to visual media than those who knew no other preaching model and, therefore, made a Christian commitment after coming to New Hope? An examination of the research data related to respondent commitment indicated statistically significant findings to this question on all three media scales. Those who made Christian commitments after attending New Hope consistently scored higher on all three media scales than those who committed themselves to

Christ prior to their attendance at the same church. Table 22 outlines the survey data for the Media Scale

(t=-2.80; df=107; p≤.01), the Pastoral Media Subscale (t=-1.98; df=107; p≤.05), and the Media Imagery Subscale (t=-2.94; df=107; p≤.01).

Table 22. Commitment and Media Receptivity

Scales	Prior Commitment			Subsequent Commitment		
	n	Mean	SD	n	Mean	SD
Media Scale	89	5.37	.98	20	6.01	.49
Pastoral Media Subscale	89	5.87	1.28	20	6.44	.53
Media Imagery Subscale	89	4.97	.98	20	5.65	.70

Summary of Significant Findings

The following summation centers in most cases on research findings that were deemed statistically significant. In several cases, especially as they related to demographic characteristics, the lack of a statistically significant finding became an important validation because it contradicts several popularly held notions about preaching today. For purposes of review, as well as further synthesis in the final chapter of this dissertation, the following summary collates eleven research findings into four broad categories based on demographic, parishioner, dogmatic, and postliterate characteristics.

Demographic Characteristics

1. Age was not a significant factor in accounting for differences between mean scores on dogmatism, the Postmodern Subjectivity Subscale, or the Media Scale.

2. Gender did not play a significant part in determining a respondent's score on any of the three media scales used in the study. While women scored

slightly higher on all three media scales, these differences were not deemed statistically significant.

Parishioner Characteristics

3. Those who made a commitment to Christ after arriving at New Hope Church scored significantly higher on all three media scales than those who made a faith commitment prior to attending the same church.

4. By the same token, no significant difference existed between mean scores on the same three media scales for those who attended New Hope prior to my introduction of visual media in 1999 and for those who began attending afterward.

5. Regarding attendance at New Hope Church, a significant correlation was found between respondent attendance patterns and mean scores on all three media scales.

Dogmatic Characteristics

6. A statistically significant negative relationship was discovered between the Pastoral Media Subscale and respondent dogmatism. The analysis revealed that respondents who scored high on dogmatism tended to score lower on the Pastoral Media Subscale; likewise, those who tended to be more open to change at New Hope also indicated a higher level of receptivity to me as their pastor and my use of visual media in preaching.

7. The data revealed a surprising and statistically significant finding that dogmatism increased in relation to respondent postliteracy.

Postliterate Characteristics

8. Based on responses categorized by age, no significant difference could be found to account for respondent preferences for either image-based or textually based memory triggers. Respondent age did not play a significant part in people's tendencies to trigger their memory either by images or text.

9. The survey data do not support a significantly clear connection between age and sermon retention. Respondent age did not account for any particular preference to recall my sermons by either visual illustration or story.

10. Not surprisingly, those who preferred news sources such as television and

the Internet also scored significantly higher on the Media Imagery Subscale than those who preferred more literate media forms.

11. Significant inverse relationships existed between mean scores on the Media Scale and the Postmodern Subjectivity Subscale and the Media Imagery Subscale as they related to respondent preferences for textual triggers in sermon retention.

CHAPTER FIVE

SUMMARY AND CONCLUSIONS

This study was initially fueled by the observed disparity between previously held assumptions about those who would most likely prefer visual media in preaching and those who actually welcomed it in my ministry context. The final chapter of this dissertation clusters the major research findings according to demographic, parishioner, dogmatic, and postliterate characteristics. Following a discussion of the major findings, the study responds to each research question with a succinct research answer, outlines the limitations of the study, offers implications of the findings and practical applications as well as contributions to research methodology, and finally offers a number of suggestions for further research.

Major Findings

Examining demographic, parishioner, dogmatic, and postliterate characteristics, this section outlines the study's major research findings.

Demographic Characteristics

Contrary to popular opinion, age was not a significant factor in accounting for differences among mean scores on dogmatism, the Postmodern Subjectivity Subscale, or the Media Scale. Based on the survey findings, preachers should not assume that age alone will necessarily cause worshipers to be more or less dogmatic, postmodern, subjective, or receptive to the use of visual media in preaching. This discovery runs contrary to much of the popular teaching at pastors' conferences and articles in ministry magazines today. Preachers should be cautious about presuming that preaching forms utilizing visual media will be more or less attractive to particular age groups.

By the same token, no significant difference could be found, based on age, to account for respondents' use of either image-based or textually based memory triggers. As a cognitive function, memory triggers do not appear to be age related. Preachers should not necessarily assume that older worshipers will prefer textually based memory triggers nor conclude that younger worshipers will naturally prefer image-based ones. Despite age, the human creation remains far more dynamic than static. This presumption, while popularly held in postmodern preaching circles, lacks statistical support in this study.

Furthermore, the survey data do not support a significantly clear connection between age and sermon retention. Preachers ought not to assume that younger worshipers are more likely to remember a pastor's visual illustration or that older worshipers are more prone to recall a pastor's story from memory. In this study, retention defies narrow age or generational groupings since more than three-quarters of all respondents preferred visual memory triggers.

Finally, the research findings indicate that gender did not play a significant part in determining a respondent's score on any of the three media scales used in the study. While women scored slightly higher on all three media scales, these differences were not statistically significant. Given the survey findings, preachers should not consider gender a dominant factor relating to a worshiper's receptivity toward the use of visual media in preaching.

Parishioner Characteristics

According to the research findings, those who made a commitment to Christ after their arrival at New Hope Church scored significantly higher on all three media scales than those who made their faith commitment prior to attending the same church. Over time, this finding may lend support to McLuhan's mantra of media becoming the message. Preachers who use visual media in their preaching should carefully consider the appetites they nurture and feed. Ongoing attention should be given to the use of media as a conveyor of biblical metaphors rather than simply a popular preaching gimmick. Those who placed their faith in Christ at New Hope showed greater receptivity to visual media in preaching than those who made their faith commitments elsewhere; the preacher's challenge is to deepen the Christian experience for all worshipers in creative, compelling ways regardless of a person's background or experience.

By the same token, the survey data showed no significant differences between mean scores on the same three media scales for those who attended New Hope prior to my introduction of electronic visual media in 1999 compared with those who came afterward. Regardless of a person's tenure at New Hope, mean scores for all three media scales were fairly high. This finding may be due in part to the strong receptivity by those who came to Christ at New Hope, as well as those who attended the church prior to the my arrival in 1999 and came to appreciate its use. For many preachers, this finding offers hope to those who fear the introduction of electronic media forms in preaching will polarize an existing congregation. The research findings indicate the opposite: no significant differences in receptivity were found in relation to congregational tenure.

The final parishioner characteristic clearly demonstrates convergent validity: regarding attendance at New Hope Church, a significant correlation existed between respondent attendance patterns and mean scores on all three media scales. Those who attended New Hope Church most regularly were also most likely to be receptive to the use of visual media in preaching. Likewise, those who attended New Hope least frequently scored the lowest means on all three media scales. Given this finding, the research could lead one to believe that the use of media itself could be the cause for less frequent attendance on the part of these individuals. By the same token, the relatively strong respondent mean scores even for those with the lowest attendance patterns indicated a good deal of support in favor of the use of visual media in preaching, thereby refuting this speculation.

Dogmatic Characteristics

The research findings indicated a statistically significant negative relationship between the Pastoral Media Subscale and respondent dogmatism. This inverse correlation can be understood in this way: as dogmatism increased, support for the pastor's use of visual media decreased. Likewise, those who tended to be more open to change also indicated a higher level of receptivity to me as their pastor and my use of visual media in preaching. On the one hand, a naturally closed individual may tend to embrace negatively worded questions like those used in this subscale more than a less dogmatic person would. On the other hand, the research indicated that those who were less dogmatic, which is to say those who were more open to change, demonstrated significant support for my use of visual media in preaching. In this case, the data reveal a negative correlation between dogmatism and respondent receptivity to the use of visual media in preaching.

I was also surprised to find that Seniors and Builders ranked highest in subjectivity according to mean scores on the Postmodern Subjectivity Subscale. The implications of this finding are surprising and potentially troubling. Does the research data actually reveal, contrary to popular opinion, that the oldest group surveyed in this study was also the most subjective? If so, what does this finding say about the extent to which postmodern subjectivity has worked its way into popular culture, including the hearts and minds of its most seasoned generations?

The second place ranking by Millennialists on the Postmodern Subjectivity Subscale was not particularly surprising; however, whether respondent subjectivity in this age group is connected in any way to youthful idealism bears further exploration. If so, then Millennial dogmatism could wane to some extent over time.

Postliterate Characteristics

The final cluster of research findings relate in a variety of ways to postliteracy. One of the most fascinating discoveries from this study was that dogmatism increased in relation to respondent postliteracy. This finding was statistically significant. Not surprisingly, the initial data corresponded with material in my literature review indicating that males tend to rate higher on dogmatism than females, with both genders rated slightly less than moderately dogmatic. However, I was shocked to find every member of the Builder and Senior generations self-selecting television as their preferred source for news. This age group was the only one to select the same form of media by every member. Perhaps the fact that the television is more readily available and likely demands the least exertion from older recipients is a consideration. Likewise, newspapers may be more difficult for some older people to read; radio may be challenging for some to hear; and the Internet requires some degree of technical sophistication to probe for news. Clearly, television is the dominant media form across the age spectrum, and this preference will continue to impact the ministry of preaching well into the future. Preachers should not be surprised to learn that those who preferred more postliterate news sources such as television and the Internet also scored significantly higher on the Media Imagery Subscale than those who preferred more literate media forms like radio or newspapers.

Earlier in this discussion, I found that no significant difference could be found, based on age, to account for respondents to use either image-based or textually based memory triggers. By the same token, the research findings indicated that, in fact, significant inverse relationships between the mean scores on the Media Scale and the Postmodern Subjectivity and Media Imagery Subscale scores regarding respondent preference for textual triggers on sermon retention. In this study, a respondent's preference for textual memory triggers decreased as subjectivity increased. Likewise, respondents who scored higher on the Media Scale and Media Imagery Subscale were less prone to use textual memory triggers. While the final two findings have coherent validity, the first finding bears further study. Why were respondents who were naturally more subjective also less likely to use textual memory triggers? The finding is not only statistically significant but also an interesting topic for further study.

Research Questions and Answers

The following section addresses each research question with a corresponding answer based on the findings of the study.

Research Question #1

How open or closed to change are survey respondents based on their responses to the Modified Rokeach E?

Research answer #1. The research data indicate that the mean score for all respondents on dogmatism was 3.71 (SD=.69), placing them near the middle of a seven-point Likert scale. According to Table 9, Millenialists ranked most dogmatic, followed by Seniors and Builders. Baby Boomers came in third place, while Baby Busters scored least dogmatic of all generational groups. Validating an earlier finding in the literature review, men scored slightly more dogmatic than women.

Research Question #2

To what degree are survey respondents either modern or postmodern in their orientation to culture?

Research answer #2. Given the natural disinclination of postmodern individuals to be categorized, this question became the most difficult one to answer in the entire study. The lack of a statistically reliable postmodern scale made this even more challenging. Perhaps Lyotard's definition of postmodernism, which emphasizes a tolerance for ambiguity, exacerbates and illustrates the problem. An analysis of the Postmodern Values Questionnaire in Section Four of the research instrument indicated that it was statistically unreliable. However, a Varimax rotation identified one construct related to postmodern subjectivity with improved, yet still statistically weak, reliability. Nevertheless, I used the data from this newfound subscale to attempt an answer to at least one facet of the research question relating specifically to respondent subjectivity.

The research data indicate that the mean score for all respondents on the Postmodern Subjectivity Subscale was 3.83 (SD=1.35), placing them very near the center of a seven-point Likert scale. Women scored slightly higher in subjectivity than men. Surprisingly, the Senior and Builder generations scored highest on the Postmodern Subjectivity Subscale, followed by the Millenialists, Baby Boomers, and Baby Busters. Since the majority of respondents were either Seniors, Builders, or Baby Boomers, many would suspect that the Postmodern Subjectivity Subscale would be lower; however, the data seemed to indicate that the postmodern trait of subjectivity was sufficiently exhibited in each generational group surveyed.

Research Question #3

How receptive are survey respondents to the use of visual media in preaching?

Research answer #3. After more than four years of using visual media at New Hope Church, congregational receptivity to its use in preaching was quite high. The research data reported a mean score for all respondents on the Media Scale of 5.49 (SD=.94). Using a seven-point Likert scale, the average for all respondents was on the upper end of the continuum. Baby Busters scored highest on the Media Scale, followed by Millenialists, Baby Boomers, and the oldest generational group, Seniors and Builders. Those who made a commitment to Christ prior to attending New Hope scored lower on the Media Scale than those who made a faith commitment after arriving at the church.

Research Question #4

Fourth, to what extent are respondents postliterate and how does postliteracy relate to their receptivity to the use of visual media in preaching?

Research answer #4. According to the research findings, approximately three-quarters of all respondents self-described themselves as preferring image-based memory triggers, regardless of age. Likewise, nearly two-thirds of all respondents indicated that television was their preferred media form for news. The data indicate a surprising discovery that Senior and Builder respondents were the only generational group to select television as their preferred news source unanimously. As a whole, newspapers ranked last, or at least near the bottom, as respondents' least favorable form of news media. Baby Boomers were more inclined to choose the Internet as their primary media form than any other generational group, yet even in this case it still came in an overwhelmingly distant second to television overall. The data indicate that television is clearly a dominant media form in every generational group. Postliteracy is not only prevalent but also transgenerational.

Years before, I assumed that younger respondents would more likely be visually oriented than their older counterparts. I thought that younger respondents would be more likely to retain sermon information on the basis of image rather than story. This assumption did not appear to bear out in the research project itself. More than half of all respondents indicated their preference to recall my past sermons by remembering a visual illustration I used, while roughly 40 percent were more likely to remember a story. Ironically, in every generational group except the Millenialists, respondents were more likely to remember my past sermons by recalling visual illustrations rather than stories I told in particular. Older respondents did not tend to favor stories over visuals more so than any other generational group.

The data also revealed a surprising finding in Table 18 (see p. 105) that dogmatism increased with postliteracy. A regression analysis revealed that a respondent's dogmatism contributed more to variance within the Pastoral Media Subscale than any other variable. The degree to which people were postliterate in their retention of sermon information was also a unique contributing factor, although to a lesser degree than dogmatism.

Research Question #5

What other variables might correlate with participant responses to the use of visual media in preaching?

Research answer #5. According to the survey findings, gender and congregational tenure did not play significant roles in respondent receptivity to the use of visual media in preaching. By the same token, statistically significant findings were identified in two areas: first, those who attended New Hope most regularly preferred the use of visual media in preaching more than those who attended the same church less often; and second, those who made a commitment to Christ prior to attending New Hope were less receptive to visual media than those who knew no other preaching model because they made their faith commitment at the same church.

Limitations of the Study

Every research study is a work-in-process offering observations and analyses from a particular historical and cultural context. As such, each one offers both strengths and weaknesses. This study is no exception. Undoubtedly, I believe this study could have been strengthened by using a longitudinal pretest-posttest design in the experimental mode rather than a nonexperimental cross-sectional analysis as was used in this study. Given the fact that I began using electronic visual media in my preaching at the outset of my ministry at New Hope in 1999, a baseline measure was no longer available for use in my ministry context, necessitating a cross-sectional design methodology rather than a more longitudinal one consisting of a baseline, treatment, and assessment. A one-year longitudinal study in a congregation that was initially unfamiliar with the use of visual media could offer researchers additional insights into any potential changes that occurred within respondents during the course of their research, particularly if a series of mid-tests were also introduced after three, six, and nine months. These insights could offer even greater insight into the ways respondents change in response to a preacher's use of visual media in preaching.

Another limitation of this study relates to the low reliability coefficient for the Postmodern Subjectivity Subscale and the even lower Cronbach alpha on the Postmodern Values Questionnaire in general. This study could have benefited greatly from a stronger scale related to the constructs comprising postmodernism. The scale used in Section Four of the survey instrument did not have sufficient internal consistency to support a reliable analysis. Further testing and development needs to be done to develop a suitable scale for use in studying postmodern attributes. The lack of a reliable scale is not only a limitation of the study but also a great opportunity for future research and is discussed at greater length later in this chapter.

Implications of the Findings and Practical Applications

The implications of this study will likely become increasingly pertinent to the practice of ministry as the postmodern cultural era continues to emerge. This discovery may be particularly true for those who serve in intergenerational ministry settings and those who may be tempted to believe that preaching that employs visually oriented elements is best suited for younger audiences primarily. In such cases, the findings from this study offer preachers some surprising insights to several commonly held assumptions about the uses of visual media in preaching. Building on the findings of this study, I hope that twenty-first-century preachers will find encouragement and counsel in the following practical applications related to the inclusion of visual media in preaching. I offer three applications for preachers who wish to benefit from the findings of this study.

Media as an Apostolic Successor of Image Bearing

First, preachers should recognize that the use of electronic visual media in preaching is a contemporary extension of the developing use of imagery in the ongoing history of the Christian Church. In the same way that Old Testament artisans like Bezalel fashioned artistic symbols to inspire Israelite worship, or Jesus himself used everyday objects like fish, bread, and water to communicate divine truth, or the Apostle Paul communicated his missionary message by finding positive points of contact within the worldview of his audiences, twenty-first-century preachers follow in an apostolic succession of image bearers, inspiring men and women to bare their hearts to God and welcome the imprinting of his image on their lives. This study reminds even the most imaginative preachers today that their creative work is not new; twenty-first-century preachers are the torchbearers of two millennia of men and women before them who used every creative means possible to communicate the Creator's great message of good news. Like Glenn Chaffee, who was introduced in Chapter 1 of this study, everyone needs to hear the divine reminder, "I AM here, too." This study underscores the prevenient creativity of the First Artist. It offers inspiration to twenty-first-century preachers who carry the torch of creative communication on behalf of those who have gone before them and for the benefit of those they presently serve.

Media as a Contextual Carrier of Biblical Metaphors

Second, this study offers a word of caution to preachers who may be prone to believe that the addition of technology alone can somehow make preaching more powerful, attractive, or contemporary. The discoveries gleaned from this study refute this popular assumption in no uncertain terms. Instead, the data indicate that preachers themselves are likely to exert more influence over congregational receptivity to the use of visual media in preaching than anything else. I suspect that pastors who weave visual media into the warp and woof of not only the sermon but also the entire worship encounter are more likely to find correspondingly higher Postmodern Media Subscale scores than those who simply use visual media for illustrative purposes. Likewise, preachers must recognize the importance of contextual coherence in both their sermons and visual media forms or they run the risk of elevating media over message. Those who use visual media in preaching must never forget this inherent danger of imagery: often, more than one story is caught by the viewers' eyes. Context is critical, both scripturally and visually. Preachers who are not visually attuned should learn to strengthen this area of weakness in themselves before attempting to preach with electronic visual media. Those who take the bait of the "PowerPointers" and assume that a projector and screen will somehow make their preaching come alive will likely become discouraged, ultimately disappointing the very people they sought to inspire. Technology alone will not make poor preachers good. Likewise, technology offers no hope of making good preachers great unless the power of a biblical metaphor finds dominance in the sermon, in the corresponding visual message that is being communicated, and in the communicators themselves. Sermons driven by a dominant biblical metaphor have power in a visually-attuned congregation. Media can communicate biblical truth as modern-day counterparts to ancient stained glass. Those who use media because it is trendy, or for presentation purposes only, will do so at great risk to themselves, their ministries, their message, and their congregations. I cannot emphasize this implication any more vehemently.

Media as Cultural Language

Finally, this study denies the commonly held notion that visual media is primarily a method for connecting with younger generations or that it is better suited for those who are not yet followers of Jesus Christ. The research data indicate that, contrary to popular opinion, men and women of all ages can be receptive to the use of visual media in preaching, regardless of their years of church experience. Preachers today cannot afford to choose either a model that connects only with those who are left- or right-brain hemisphere dominant. Babin and Iannone's admonition of stereo catechesis is an appropriate example of preaching in the emerging postmodern age. This study found that most men and women, regardless of their age, indicated a relatively high level of receptivity to the use of visual media in preaching in the researcher's own ministry context. Most of these individuals never experienced preaching with electronic visual media prior to their exposure to it at New Hope Church. Contrary to popular opinion, receptivity to its use was not dependent on age, gender, or church experience.

Contributions to Research Methodology

The greatest contribution this study makes to research methodology involves the use of the Pastoral Media Subscale and its implications both for future research and for the task of preaching in an increasingly visual culture. This subscale was serendipitously discovered during the data analysis phase of the project rather than by my intent or design. It indicates that pastors themselves play a key role in influencing congregational receptivity to the use of visual media in preaching. The research findings indicate that congregational receptiveness to contemporary preaching forms still hinges in large measure on the integrity and commitment of the preacher; no amount of technology can make up for this vital factor. Preachers cannot give their media teams an outline or manuscript for their sermons and simply expect them to build visual presentations in support of them. Preachers who have such expectations yet continue to preach in a preferred modern or literate style that is geared primarily to a speaker and listening audience will likely face personal disappointment and congregational frustration. Those who fail to recognize their key role as personal integrators of both the biblical message and communication methodology risk conveying dissonance and incoherence because of the bifurcation of what is seen and heard. Failure to recognize this truth can lead to congregational misinterpretation of the biblical message, or the visual media form, or both. Instead, preachers who desire to develop a visual homiletic must first identify a central biblical metaphor as part of their exegesis for use in their preaching and graphic representations. Without this, the preacher runs the very real risk of eisegesis. The Pastoral Media Subscale underscores the importance of the preacher and his or her role as a personal agent of communicating the central message of this graphic gospel in creative, compelling, and contemporary ways.

Suggestions for Further Study

Without question, the challenge related to the development of a scale for postmodernism is daunting, especially given the inherent reluctance of postmodern individuals to be categorized. Despite this assessment, future research in this area could be aided by the development of a statistically standardized scale that addresses postmodernism as a general category. More likely, further research would first need to center on the underlying constructs that make up postmodernism, exploring issues like community, disillusionment, diversity, subjective experience, and the influence of media in greater depth. I hope that the Postmodern Subjectivity Subscale used in this study could serve as a foundational tool upon which a more reliable scale could be built.

A surprising insight from the research findings stems from the correlation between dogmatism and postliteracy. Why were the study's most dogmatic respondents, who were themselves the most resistant to change, unanimously committed to a more postliterate media form like television? Prior to the study, I suspected that respondents who scored higher on dogmatism would also be more likely to prefer more traditionally literate news media forms, especially the newspaper. The survey data did not correlate with the researcher's hypothesis. Future research could uncover why this hypothesis was not confirmed.

Another question growing out of the research findings involves the correlation between dogmatism and postliteracy. If dogmatism increases with postliteracy, as seen in the research findings, how might this finding shape the church's use of technology? A third area where further research bears attention is an examination of dogmatism among Millenialists. What inherent qualities exist within Millenialists that led them to score higher than any other generational group on dogmatism? Can their dogmatism be traced to Millenialists as a distinct generational group, or was this finding related to a particular developmental stage in which respondents found themselves at the time of the study?

Likewise, further research could be conducted on why Postmodern Subjectivity Subscale scores at New Hope Church increased with age. Does subjectivity increase with respondent age? Have earlier studies found a correlation between subjectivity in general and aging? What insights could be gleaned from the discipline of developmental psychology in respect to these questions? Does this research finding indicate that the postmodern construct of subjectivity is so pervasive in the culture already that in this case it has gained its greatest strength in the oldest generational group involved in the study?

Finally, I hope that all three media scales from this study, each of which evidenced high degrees of reliability, could serve as a foundation for further study in this dynamic area of social research in pastoral ministry. The use of visual media in preaching is not likely to wane in my opinion; more and more churches today recognize a need to engage more of the senses in worship and preaching. However, churches and the pastors who lead them need to do more than simply "get a screen" or "go digital." I hope that the media scales developed for this study could help churches recognize their own potential receptivity to visual media based on their own level of dogmatism. In addition, the Pastoral Media Subscale offers potential for understanding congregational perceptions about the preachers' commitment to the use of visual exegesis in their preaching and also helps these preachers themselves discover if they are personally communicating a faithful integration of the biblical message through visual elements in their preaching.

By the same token, the Postmodern Subjectivity Subscale could offer potential either as an existing scale, provided further testing indicated greater reliability among other survey populations, or for use as a starting point upon which a stronger research scale could be built. Regardless, I would take great pride in learning that these findings served as a foundation for further work in these important areas of study.

Postscript

For more than five years now, I have imagined countless times how it would feel to write the concluding paragraphs in this dissertation. Indeed, at many points I doubted the very possibility. This journey has undoubtedly taken me in many directions across rocky roads, along winding paths, and even through a number of boggy places and thorny patches. At several points, dead ends stopped me in my tracks. A very serious family illness, the demands of a growing church, and the pressures of serving as general contractor for an eight thousand square-foot, first-phase building program hampered my efforts. My own need to nurture my marriage and raise three young daughters rightfully competed for a great deal of my time and energy. Nevertheless, God's faithfulness empowered me to return again to the task of completing this dissertation and enable my family and congregation to support my efforts. Just as significantly, and perhaps even more miraculous, divine grace inspired me to fall in love with the research itself.

The call to preach is ominous. Men and women are not only able to respond; Jesus' mandate calls us to do so responsibly. In an age when much of the media used today in churches is anecdotal or incidental, I challenge preachers to develop a visual hermeneutic that grounds, frames, and shields their visual homiletic. At this point, I would be especially gratified if this work served as a catalyst for further study, inspiring churches and preachers alike to convey the life-changing message of the gospel in the most creative and compelling means possible. I offer this work for God's glory alone: "*Soli Deo Glori.*"

APPENDIX A

The Research Instrument

Cover Letter

21 September 2003

Dear Members and Friends of New Hope Church,

Most of you are aware that I am moving into the final stages of my doctor of ministry studies at Asbury Theological Seminary. This survey incorporates my residential course work at Asbury from 1998-1999 as well as my experiences at New Hope over the past four years. Upon a successful defense of my dissertation, I will graduate in May 2004.

A primary element of my research focuses on a survey of our congregation's receptivity to the use of visual media. By visual media, I mean the use of video clips and graphic art presentations that are projected electronically on our large format screen. I am curious which factors in people most affect receptivity to the use of these forms of visual media in preaching.

One of the ways I will determine this receptivity is by measuring a person's relative openness to change based on responses to the survey. In section two, you will find twenty questions addressing this issue. This section in particular asks some questions that may initially catch you by surprise, including several standardized questions that relate to political concerns. Keep in mind that your survey will remain anonymous and no effort will be made to identify respondents. Please do not second-guess these questions even though most of them are not related to spiritual issues or even to the use of visual media. Nevertheless, your responses to these well-tested questions, in particular, will help me measure our congregation's relative openness to change.

The third section of the survey includes ten questions based on your observations of my use of visual media in preaching here at New Hope. Please answer each question as honestly as you can. Do not try to answer the questions the way you think I, as your pastor, would like you to answer them–just offer your best responses. Keep in mind that your first impression will often be your most honest response.

The final section of the survey raises sixteen questions addressing your personal beliefs about a number of cultural value statements. In each case, remember that I am not looking for any particular answer. Instead, I simply would like to know the degree to which you either agree or disagree with each statement. Your responses to these questions will help me assess the degree to which our congregation embraces popular culture.

The information provided through this survey will be presented to my dissertation committee at Asbury, so please do your best to answer every question as honestly as you can. All responses will be confidential, and no individual will be identified with their responses. In order to preserve everyone's confidentiality, please do <u>not</u> provide your name on this survey. You must be at least fourteen years old to participate. Submission of this survey indicates your consent to participate in the study.

In a recent pretest, most people completed the survey in less than fifteen minutes. You may complete it more or less quickly depending on the amount of time you choose to spend on each question. Please do not hurry your way through the survey; remember that this is <u>not</u> a race. Instead, you will help me most by giving yourself adequate time to answer every question as honestly as you can. In Section One, please place a check mark in the box corresponding to your preferred response. In sections two through four, circle the number that best applies to you. Use the number "4" to indicate if you are unable to answer a question. Should you change your mind on an answer, please erase it or place an "X" through it before changing your response. If possible, please answer **every** question in the survey before placing it in the offering basket in the back of our worship centre.

Your thoughtful responses are essential to the success of my research. With your assistance, this survey data may be useful in helping other preachers learn more effective ways to communicate to people of all ages. Upon final completion, I will make several copies of my completed dissertation available should anyone want to review my research findings.

Thanks again for all your help–I appreciate it so much!

Sincerely,

Jay Akkerman

Section One

Section 1: *Please respond to the multiple-choice questions in this introductory section by placing a check mark next to the answer that best describes what is true for you. All answers will remain confidential. If you need to change an answer, please erase it or place an "X" through it and then check your preferred answer. If possible, please answer every question in the entire survey.*

Questions	Answers
A. Gender	❏ Female. ❏ Male.
B. When were you born?	❏ Before 1925. ❏ Between 1925-44. ❏ Between 1945-63. ❏ Between 1964-80. ❏ After 1980.
C. Please describe your personal relationship with God.	❏ I committed my life to Christ **before** I began attending New Hope Church. ❏ I committed my life to Christ **after** attending New Hope Church.

❏ I have **not yet** made a commitment to Christ.

❏ I am **not sure** about my relationship with God.

D. Approximately how long have you attended New Hope Church?

❏ I am a first-time guest.

❏ Less than a month.

❏ One to six months.

❏ Six months to a year.

❏ One to four years.

❏ Prior to Rev. Akkerman's arrival in 1999.

E. Please describe your attendance at New Hope Church in the past six months.

❏ Nearly every week.

❏ Twice a month.

❏ Once a month.

❏ On holidays and special occasions.

F. Presuming that you had a yearbook, if you were trying to locate friends from school days whose names you forgot, would you most likely.

❏ Look for their class photos in the yearbook to trigger your memory?

❏ Scan for their names in the yearbook to trigger your memory?

G. If you wanted to learn about the news later this afternoon, which <u>one</u> method would you prefer to use?

❏ Read a newspaper.

❏ Listen to the radio.

❏ Watch television.

❏ Check an Internet site.

H. When you think about one of Pastor Jay's past sermons, which are you more likely to remember?

❏ Stories he told in particular.

❏ A visual illustration he used to make his point.

Section Two

Section 2: *Please <u>circle the best answer</u> to indicate the degree to which you agree or disagree with each of the following twenty statements related to your relative openness to change. Please answer every question as honestly as possible. If you are unable to decide an answer, please circle the number "4." If you need to correct an answer, place erase it or place an "X" over the wrong answer and try again.*

	Strongly Disagree						Strongly
A. The United States and Iraq have just about nothing in common.	1	2	3	4	5	6	7
B. The highest form of government is a democracy, and the highest form of democracy is a government run by those who are most intelligent.	1	2	3	4	5	6	7
C. Even though freedom of speech for all groups is a worthwhile goal, it is unfortunately necessary to restrict the freedom of certain political groups.	1	2	3	4	5	6	7
D. On our own, we are helpless and miserable creatures.	1	2	3	4	5	6	7
E. Most people just don't care for others.	1	2	3	4	5	6	7

F. I'd like it if I could find someone who would tell me how to solve my personal problems.   1   2   3   4   5   6   7

G. In a discussion I often find it necessary to repeat myself several times to make sure I am being understood.   1   2   3   4   5   6   7

H. It is better to be a dead hero than a live coward.   1   2   3   4   5   6   7

I. While I don't even like to admit this even to myself, my secret ambition is to become a great person, like Einstein or Beethoven or Shakespeare.   1   2   3   4   5   6   7

J. The main thing in life is for a person to want to do something important.   1   2   3   4   5   6   7

K. It is only when people devote themselves to an ideal or cause that life becomes meaningful.   1   2   3   4   5   6   7

L. Of all the different philosophies that exist in this world, there is probably only one that is correct.	1	2	3	4	5	6	7
M. To compromise with our political opponents is dangerous because it usually leads to a betrayal of our own side.	1	2	3	4	5	6	7
N. There are two kinds of people in this world: those who are for the truth and those who are against the truth.	1	2	3	4	5	6	7
O. My blood boils whenever people stubbornly refuse to admit they are wrong.	1	2	3	4	5	6	7
P. Most of the ideas that get printed nowadays aren't worth the paper they are printed on.	1	2	3	4	5	6	7
Q. In this complicated world of ours, the only way we can know what's going on is to rely on leaders or experts who can be trusted.	1	2	3	4	5	6	7
R. It is often desirable to reserve judgment about what's going on until	1	2	3	4	5	6	7

we have had a chance to hear the opinions of those we respect.

S. The *present* is all too often full of unhappiness—it's only the *future* that counts.   1   2   3   4   5   6   7

T. Most people just don't know what's good for them.   1   2   3   4   5   6   7

Section Three

Section 3: *Please <u>circle the best answer</u> to each of the following questions based on your personal beliefs and observations of the pastor's use of visual media (e.g., video clips and graphic images) in preaching at New Hope Church. Remember that your first impression is often your most honest response to each question.*

	Strongly Disagree						Strongly
A. Images are nice in sermons, but words really get the point across to me.	1	2	3	4	5	6	7
B. A picture really is worth a thousand words, even in a sermon.	1	2	3	4	5	6	7
C. I have been emotionally moved by the use of visual media in a sermon.	1	2	3	4	5	6	7
D. Jesus used the visual methods of his day in his communication.	1	2	3	4	5	6	7
E. Generally, I find the pastor's use of visual media distracting.	1	2	3	4	5	6	7
F. Using visual media in preaching today is a gimmick.	1	2	3	4	5	6	7

G. I suspect the pastor likely chooses video clips **before** selecting his Bible text.   1   2   3   4   5   6   7

H. My friends would likely find our church's use of visual media interesting.   1   2   3   4   5   6   7

I. Often, the visual media used in the sermon do not relate to the Bible text.   1   2   3   4   5   6   7

J. I like visual media because it is easier for me to see the screen than to read.   1   2   3   4   5   6   7

K. I wish the pastor would stop using visual media in his preaching.   1   2   3   4   5   6   7

Section Four

Section 4: *For this final section, please <u>circle the best answer</u> to each of the following questions based on your personal beliefs about the following cultural value statements. Thanks for your candid responses.*

	Strongly Disagree						Strongly
A. I believe honesty is always the right policy, even if the truth hurts.	1	2	3	4	5	6	7
B. Just give me the facts.	1	2	3	4	5	6	7
C. I am optimistic about the future.	1	2	3	4	5	6	7
D. Having friends to rely on is very important to me.	1	2	3	4	5	6	7
E. Truth can vary based on the individual.	1	2	3	4	5	6	7
F. For news, I prefer a newspaper over a television.	1	2	3	4	5	6	7

G. I always consult my friends when deciding between right and wrong.	1	2	3	4	5	6	7
H. Show me, don't tell me.	1	2	3	4	5	6	7
I. It is difficult to be certain about much of anything today.	1	2	3	4	5	6	7
J. It is impossible for a juror to be objective.	1	2	3	4	5	6	7
K. It is alright for men and women to share the same cologne fragrance.	1	2	3	4	5	6	7
L. I prefer to say that something is "appropriate" rather than if it is "right."	1	2	3	4	5	6	7
M. I'm not much of a reader.	1	2	3	4	5	6	7
N. I am confident that the world's complex issues can be worked out.	1	2	3	4	5	6	7
O. I am the same person I was yesterday.	1	2	3	4	5	6	7

P. For information, I prefer the Internet rather than the television.   1   2   3   4   5   6   7

Thanks! Please place your completed survey in the offering basket in the back of our worship centre.

APPENDIX B

The Huckins Postmodern Identification Questionnaire

	Strongly Disagree				Strongly Agree	
A. I believe it is never right to be dishonest.	1	2	3	4	5	6
B. When making decisions I only consider the facts.	1	2	3	4	5	6
C. I feel optimistic about the future.	1	2	3	4	5	6
D. I make moral choices on my own, regardless of what others may think or say.	1	2	3	4	5	6
E. My "family" includes my friends and others close to me.	1	2	3	4	5	6
F. What I see and feel is what I believe.	1	2	3	4	5	6

G. When I have to make a choice about a moral issue, I believe it is more important to be practical than right.   1   2   3   4   5   6

H. I can learn all I need to know about the world through the news media.   1   2   3   4   5   6

I. I always consult my friends when I'm trying to decide between right and wrong.   1   2   3   4   5   6

J. I am not confident the complex issues we face today can be worked out.   1   2   3   4   5   6

K. I feel that being honest is always right even if it hurts another person.   1   2   3   4   5   6

L. I believe the media has a strong influence in my life.   1   2   3   4   5   6

M. I find great satisfaction from just being with my friends.   1   2   3   4   5   6

APPENDIX C

The Steele-Drovdahl-Grenz Postmodern Survey

Are you Modern or Postmodern?

What do you think?

1. Interpreting is more important than knowing. — I agree / I disagree

2. It was impossible for the O. J. Simpson jury to be objective. — I agree / I disagree

3. Reality is socially constructed. — I agree / I disagree

4. Perception is reality. — I agree / I disagree

5. MTV is cool. — I agree / I disagree

6. I believe in timeless truth. — I agree / I disagree

7. I prefer realism in art. — I agree / I disagree

8. Classical music is the finest music ever composed.	I agree	I disagree
9. The meaning of most biblical texts is self-evident.	I agree	I disagree
10. "I" exist separate from my body.	I agree	I disagree
11. I prefer "appropriate" to "right" and "inappropriate" to "wrong."	I agree	I disagree
12. We need to "celebrate the differences" in people.	I agree	I disagree
13. Remember: there is always another story.	I agree	I disagree
14. Think globally; act locally.	I agree	I disagree
15. Identity crises are passé.	I agree	I disagree
16. I'm optimistic about social progress.	I agree	I disagree

17. Men and women should not share the same cologne.	I agree	I disagree
18. It's possible to know the truth.	I agree	I disagree
19. I am the same person I was yesterday.	I agree	I disagree
20. Knowledge is values-free.	I agree	I disagree
21. The new interest in spirituality is good.	I agree	I disagree
22. The Church needs to adapt to culture.	I agree	I disagree

APPENDIX D

Parental Consent Form

21 September 2003

Dear Parent,

Most of you are aware that I am moving into the final stages of my doctor of ministry studies at Asbury Theological Seminary. Upon a successful defense of my dissertation, I will graduate in May 2004.

A major element of my research focuses on a survey of our congregation at New Hope Church and their receptivity to the use of visual media. By visual media, I mean the use of video clips and graphic art presentations that are projected electronically on our large format screen. I am curious which factors in people of all ages most affect receptivity to the use of these forms of visual media in preaching.

Because I would like the broadest age representation possible, I am requesting your adolescent's participation in the study. This participation involves the completion of the enclosed four-page survey booklet. Your child's participation in this study is voluntary. You are free to choose not to have your adolescent participate. Likewise, if your child chooses not to participate, these decisions will not adversely affect you, your child, or your relationship to me as pastor or to New Hope in general.

If you have any questions concerning my research study or your child's participation in it, you may reach me at the church at 480.785.9500 and I will be happy to more fully answer any questions you may have. The cover letter to the enclosed survey also provides additional information you may find helpful.

To give consent, please sign and date the section below. To ensure respondent confidentiality, please seal the consent form in the small enclosed white envelope and then place it in the larger manila envelope with your child's completed survey. To facilitate data entry, please return these items to me in person or via the mail by Wednesday, 1 October 2003. Thanks for your help–I really appreciate it!

Sincerely,

Jay Akkerman

I give consent for my child to participate in Pastor Jay Akkerman's doctor of ministry research study and understand that his or her participation in this study is voluntary.

_____ _____ _____

Parent Signature   Child's Name–please print   Date

WORKS CITED

Achtemeier, Paul J. "*Omne Verbum Sonat:* The New Testament and the Oral Environment of Late Western Antiquity." *Journal of Biblical Literature* 109 (1990): 3-27.

Adult Education and Family Literacy Act of 1998. Pub. L. 105-220. 7 Aug. 1998. Stat. 1061. 7 Sept. 2003 <http://frwebgate.access.gpo.gov/cgi-bin/getdoc.cgi?dbname= 105_cong_public_laws&docid=f:publ220.105>.

Babin, Pierre and Mercedes Iannone. *The New Era in Religious Communication.* Minneapolis: Fortress, 1991.

Barna, George. *The Barna Report.* Ventura, CA: Regal, 1992.

---. *The Second Coming of the Church.* Nashville: Word, 1998.

Bartlett, Michael. "The Future of News: Interactive News on the Tube." *USC Annenberg Online Journalism Review* 10 Jul. 2003: 44 pars. 9 Jul. 2003 <http://www.ojr.org/ojr/future/1024607102.php>.

Baxandall, Michael. *Painting and Experience in Fifteenth Century Italy.* New York: Oxford UP, 1972.

Beaudoin, Tom. *Virtual Faith: The Irreverent Spiritual Quest of Generation X.* San Francisco: Jossey-Bass, 1998.

Bevan, Edwyn. *Holy Images: An Inquiry into Idolatry and Image-Worship in Ancient Paganism and in Christianity.* London: Unwin, 1940.

Biggers, Julian L. "An A Priori Approach for Developing Short-Forms of Tests and Inventories." *Journal of Experimental Education* 44 (Spring 1976): 8-10.

Boomershine, Thomas E. Foreword. *Thinking in Story: Preaching in a Post-Literate Age.* By Richard A. Jensen. Lima, OH: C. S. S., 1993. 13.

---. "Peter's Denial as Polemic or Confession: The Implications of Media Criticism for Biblical Hermeneutics." *Semeia* 39 (1987): 47-68.

Brooks, Phillips. *The Joy of Preaching.* Grand Rapids: Kregel, 1989.

Brueggemann, Walter. *Finally Comes the Poet: Daring Speech for Proclamation*. Philadelphia: Fortress, 1989.

---. *Texts Under Negotiation: The Bible and Postmodern Imagination*. Minneapolis: Fortress, 1993.

Buechner, Frederick. *The Faces of Jesus*. New York: Riverwood-Simon, 1974.

Buttrick, David. *Homiletic: Moves and Structures*. Philadelphia: Fortress, 1987.

Cahoone, Lawrence, ed. *From Modernism to Postmodernism*. Malden, MA: Blackwell, 2003.

Celek, Tim, and Dieter Zander. *Inside the Soul of a New Generation*. Grand Rapids: Zondervan, 1996.

Clendenin, Daniel B. "From the Verbal to the Visual: Orthodox Icons and the Sanctification of Sight." *Christian Scholars Review* 25 (Sept. 1995): 30-46.

Clines, Paul D. "Preaching for Discipleship in an Emerging Postmodern Culture." Diss. Asbury Theological Seminary, 1999.

Davey, Randall E. "The Cinema." *The Preacher's Magazine* 62.4 (June/July/Aug. 1987): 27+.

Dickens, Arthur Geoffrey. *Reformation and Society in Sixteenth Century Europe*. New York: Harcourt, 1966.

Diebold, William J. *Word and Image*. Boulder, CO: Westview, 2000.

Easum, Bill. Foreword. *Digital Storytellers*. By Len Wilson and Jason Moore. Nashville: Abingdon, 2002. 11.

Epstein, Jason. *Book Business: Publishing Past, Present, and Future*. New York: Norton, 2001.

Erickson, Millard J. *The New Evangelical Theology*. Westwood, NJ: Revell, 1968.

Farhi, Paul. "Good News for 'McPaper.'" *Washington Business Journal* 11 Aug. 1997 : 12-14.

Gannett. "Company History." 42 pars. 3 Sept. 1998 <http://www.gannett.com/map/history.htm>.

Gates, Dominic. "The Future of the News: Newspapers in the Digital Age." *USC Annenberg Online Journalism Review* 1 May 2002 : 52 pars. 12 Jul. 2003

<http://www.ojr.org/ojr/future/1020298748.php>.

Gilmore, Myron P. *The World of Humanism, 1453-1517*. New York: Harper, 1952.

Goethals, Gregor T. *The Electronic Golden Calf: Images, Religion, and the Making of Meaning*. Cambridge, MA: Cowley, 1990.

Gooden, C. Mark. "Preaching Doctrine in a Postmodern World." Diss. Asbury Theological Seminary, 2003.

Green, Joel B., and Mark D. Baker. *Recovering the Scandal of the Cross: Atonement in New Testament and Contemporary Contexts*. Downers Grove, IL: InterVarsity, 2000.

Greidanus, Sidney. *The Modern Preacher and the Ancient Text*. Grand Rapids: Eerdmans, 1988.

Grenz, Stanley J. *A Primer on Postmodernism*. Grand Rapids: Eerdmans, 1996.

Grider, J. Kenneth. "Incarnation." *Beacon Dictionary of Theology*. Ed. Richard S. Taylor. Kansas City: Beacon Hill, 1983. 279-80.

Hill, Peter C. "The Dogmatism Scale." *Measures of Religiosity*. Ed. Peter C. Hill and Ralph W. Hood. Birmingham: Religious Education P, 1999. 490-93.

Holy Bible, New International Version. Grand Rapids: Zondervan, 1973.

Huckins, Daniel J. "The Impact of Biblical Preaching on the Life of the Religious Seeker." Diss. Asbury Theological Seminary, 1998.

Ingersol, Stan. Telephone interview. 13 Oct. 2003.

Jensen, Richard A. *Thinking in Story: Preaching in a Post-Literate Age*. Lima, OH: C. S. S., 1993.

Johnston, Graham. *Preaching to a Postmodern World: A Guide to Reaching Twenty-First Century Listeners*. Grand Rapids: Baker, 2001.

Kerr, Hugh T. "In But Not of the World." *Theology Today* 15 (Oct. 1958): 293-8.

Kilde, Jeanne Halgren. *When Church Became Theatre: The Transformation of Evangelical Architecture and Worship in Nineteenth-Century America*. New York: Oxford UP, 2002.

König, Eberhard, and Gabriele Bartz. *Michelangelo*. Masters of Italian Art Series.

Cologne, Ger.: Konemann, 1998.

Lathrop, Gordon. "How Symbols Speak." *Music and the Arts in Christian Worship*. Ed. Robert E. Webber. Nashville: Star Song, 1994. Vol. 4. Book 2 of *The Complete Library of Christian Worship*. 8 vols. 1994.

Latriola, Albert C., and John W. Smeltz. *The Bible of the Poor*. Pittsburgh: Duquesne UP, 1990.

Leadership Network. "Preaching in Today's Culture." *NetFax* (12 Feb. 1999): 1-2.

"Leading with His Chin." *Charlie Rose*. Transcript. Thirteen/WNET. PBS. Journal Graphics. 18 Oct. 1996.

Lyotard, Jean- François. *The Postmodern Condition: A Report on Knowledge*. Trans. Geoff Bennington and Brian Massumi. Minneapolis: U of Minnesota P, 1984.

Manual/1976. Kansas City: Nazarene Publishing House, 1976.

Manual/2001-2005. Kansas City: Nazarene Publishing House, 2001.

Max, D. T. "The Electronic Book." *The American Scholar*. 69 (Summer 2000): 17-28.

McLuhan, Marshall. *The Gutenberg Galaxy*. Toronto: U of Toronto P, 1962.

---. *Understanding Media*. New York: McGraw, 1964.

Meyrowitz, Joshua. *No Sense of Place*. New York: Oxford UP, 1985.

Microsoft Excel. Computer software. Ver. 2002. CD-ROM. Redmond: WA: Microsoft, 2002.

Miles, Margaret R. *Image as Insight.* Boston: Beacon, 1985.

Miller, Calvin. *Marketplace Preaching.* Grand Rapids: Baker, 1995.

---. Foreword. *Reaching Generation Next.* By Lewis A. Drummond. Grand Rapids: Baker, 2002. 9.

Mouw, Richard J. *Called to Holy Worldliness.* Philadelphia: Fortress, 1980.

National Institute for Literacy. "Fast Facts on Literacy." 9 pars. 16 Mar. 1999 <http://www.nifl.gov/newworld/fastfact.htm>.

Newbigin, Lesslie. *Proper Confidence.* Grand Rapids: Eerdmans, 1995.

Oord, Thomas Jay. "Postmodernism–What Is It?" *Didache.* (Winter 2001): 14 Nov. 2003 <http://www.nazarene.org/iboe/riie/Didache/Didache_vol1_2/index.html>.

Ouspensky, Leonid, and Vladimir Lossky. *The Meaning of Icons.* Crestwood, NY: St. Vladimir's Seminary P, 1982.

Polanyi, Michael. *Personal Knowledge.* Chicago: U of Chicago P, 1974.

Pulitzer Prize Board. "The Pulitzer Prize: Nominated Finalists 2002." 44 pars. 14 Nov.

2003 <http://www.pulitzer.org/cyear/2002f.html>.

Reid, John, Lesslie Newbigin, and David Pullinger. *Modern, Postmodern and Christian.* Monrovia, CA: MARC, 1996.

Ricoeur, Paul. *The Symbolism of Evil.* Trans. Emerson Buchanan. Boston: Beacon, 1967.

Rohrbaugh, Richard, ed. *The Social Sciences and New Testament Interpretation.* Peabody, MA: Hendrickson, 1996.

Schultz, Thom, and Joani Schultz. *Why Nobody Learns Much of Anything at Church.* Loveland, CO: Group, 1993.

Schwarz, Tony. *Media: The Second God.* New York: Random, 1981.

Slaughter, Michael. *Out on the Edge*. Nashville: Abingdon, 1998.

Smith, Chuck, Jr. *The End of the World . . . As We Know It*. Colorado Springs: Waterbrook, 2001.

Smith, David F. "Can We Hear What They Heard? The Effect of Orality upon a Markan Reading-Event." Diss. U of Durham, 2002.

Staples, Rob L. *Outward Sign and Inward Grace: The Place of the Sacraments in Wesleyan Spirituality*. Kansas City: Beacon Hill, 1991.

Statistical Package for the Social Sciences. Computer software. Version 9. CD-ROM. Chicago: SPSS, 1997.

Steele, Les, and Bob Drovdahl. "Postmodernism Survey." Rev. Stanley Grenz. Classroom survey. Seattle Pacific University. 2003.

Strathern, Paul. *Foucault in 90 Minutes*. Chicago: Ivan Dee, 2000.

Sweet, Leonard. *AquaChurch*. Loveland, CO: Group, 1999.

Sweet, Leonard, Brian McLaren, and Jerry Haselmayer. *A is for Abductive*. Grand Rapids: Zondervan, 2003.

Troeger, Thomas H. *Ten Strategies for Preaching in a Multi Media Culture*. Nashville: Abingdon, 1996.

Troldahl, Verling C., and Frederic A. Powell. "A Short-Form Dogmatism Scale for Use in Field Studies." *Social Forces* 44 (Dec. 1965): 211-15.

Walker, E. F., H. B. Hosley, and E. A. Girvin, eds. *Manual of the Pentecostal Church of*

the Nazarene. Kansas City: Publishing House of the Pentecostal Church of the Nazarene, 1911.

Webber, Robert, ed. *Music and the Arts in Christian Worship*. Nashville: Star Song, 1994. Vol. 4. Book 2 of *The Complete Library of Christian Worship*. 8 vols. 1994.

---. *The Worship Phenomenon*. Nashville: Star Song, 1994.

---. *The Younger Evangelicals*. Grand Rapids: Baker, 2002.

Whitehead, Alfred North. *Symbolism: Its Meaning and Effect.* New York: Fordham UP, 1985.

Williams, James. *Lyotard: Towards a Postmodern Philosophy.* Malden, MA: Blackwell, 1998.

Wilson, Len. "Redefining Literacy: The Church in an Electronic Age." M. A. thesis. United Theological Seminary, 1995.

Wilson, Len, and Jason Moore. *Digital Storytellers.* Nashville: Abingdon, 2002.

Yaghjian, Lucretia. "Ancient Reading." *The Social Sciences and New Testament Interpretation.* Ed. Richard Rohrbaugh. Peabody, MA: Hendrickson, 1996.

Academy of Preachers

The Academy of Preachers (AoP) is a national, non-profit, trans-denominational organization with a mission to "identify, network, support, and inspire young people in their call to gospel preaching." It was launched in 2009 by Dwight A. Moody with a generous grant from the Lilly Endowment of Indianapolis, Indiana. Dr. Moody continues to serve as president of the AoP. The AoP is undergirded by the conviction that gospel preaching is socially significant vocation worthy of the very best and brightest of our young adults.

The AoP consists of an established network of denominational, congregational, and institutional partners. AoP memberships are available for Young Preachers, ($25 per year), Professional Ministers ($120) and iPartners ($500, for organizations and institutions). Members take a lead role in planning and leading campus and regional Festivals of Young Preachers and also such national AoP initiatives as the Gospel Catalyst Network, the National Festival of Young Preachers, and the coming Summer Festival of Young Preachers.

The AoP supports and sponsors Festivals for those between the ages of 14 and 28 who are exploring or embracing a call to gospel preaching. These Young Preachers preach at the Festivals, receive professional assessment, and gather for prayer and discussion with other Young Preachers. Participants are typically drawn from all traditions of Christian faith and practice, including Evangelical, Orthodox, Pentecostal, Protestant, and Roman Catholic.

Our publishing imprint, Academy of Preachers Books, seeks to publish books written by our Young Preachers in addition to this Dissertation Series for PhD and DMin manuscripts written by AoP members and friends on themes and issues related to preaching.

For more information about the Academy of Preachers, including how you can become a member, a donor, or an event host, consult one of these avenues of information.

Academy of Preachers, Inc.
150 East High Street, Lexington, Kentucky, 40507
www.academyofpreachers.net
www.youtube.com/academyofpreachers

www.ingramcontent.com/pod-product-compliance
Lightning Source LLC
Chambersburg PA
CBHW052137110526
44591CB00012B/1759